the
Postmodern
Life Cycle

the
Postmodern
Life Cycle

Challenges for Church
and Theology

Friedrich L. Schweitzer

CHALICE
PRESS

ST. LOUIS, MISSOURI

© Copyright 2004 by Friedrich L. Schweitzer

Cover art: Getty Images
Cover and interior design: Elizabeth Wright

This book is printed on acid-free, recycled paper.

Visit Chalice Press on the World Wide Web at
www.chalicepress.com

10 9 8 7 6 5 4 3 2 1   04 05 06 07 08 09

Library of Congress Cataloging–in–Publication Data

Schweitzer, Friedrich.
The postmodern life cycle : challenges for church and theology / Friedrich Schweitzer.
    p. cm.
    ISBN 0-8272-2998-4 (pbk. : alk. paper)
    1. Life cycle, Human–Religious aspects–Christianity. 2. Postmodernism–Religious aspects–Christianity. I. Title.
    BV4597.555S39 2004
    261.8–dc22

                                                    2004002457

Printed in the United States of America

Contents

Dedicated to
Princeton Theological Seminary
and to its
wonderful staff and students

Introduction

The postmodern life cycle is a topic that leads into controversies and contradictions. It is connected to deep feelings of worry and fear but also to new beginnings, hopes, and longings. It is a topic that is closely related to the work of ministers, counselors, and educators who want to address the needs of contemporary people and who want to offer support and guidance to them. All of them have to confront the challenges of the changing shape of the life cycle and the experiences of personal discontinuity in a time that has been called "postmodernity" exactly because of its discontinuous character.

Beyond professional interests and needs, any reference to the life cycle and to its religious dimension in the first place rings a bell with individual persons who, at different points of their lives and with different tasks in front of them, are wondering about the meaning of their lives. The image of a cycle is attractive and comforting. It connotes a circular form—a rounded shape that can symbolize wholeness, completion, and fulfillment. But, does this kind of circle still exist? Is it still possible to reach this kind of wholeness?

Some readers may feel challenged by the inner contradiction of the title of this book, *The Postmodern Life Cycle.* They may object to this title by pointing out that postmodernity means that everything that appeared to be stable, closed up, and fixed for good now has become open, flexible, and ready for redefinition or reconstruction. Is the reference to the postmodern life cycle a contradiction in terms? Or, not much better, is it expressive of some kind of nostalgia that is hoping to escape the pressures of postmodernity by focussing on the individual life cycle? Of course, it is also possible to read this title from the opposite point of view—the perspective not of nostalgia but of a plea for postmodern transformation. From this point of view, the reference to the postmodern life cycle could mean that we should adapt ourselves to postmodernity by accepting the biographies it offers to us and by becoming truly postmodern ourselves.

The more I became interested in such puzzling questions about the relationship between postmodernity and the life cycle, the more of a surprise it was to find out that these questions have not been treated to any major degree in the literature. Especially in practical theology and Christian education, the increasingly important concern

1

about the changing life cycle in the praxis of the church has not received sufficient attention in corresponding research and publications. But, as I want to show in this book, the postmodern life cycle is itself a theological issue in that it rests upon images and expectations that include a religious dimension. What kind of faith or religion is really guiding the postmodern life cycle? What kind of religious images does it incorporate, and how are we to judge these images from the perspective of theology? What is the contribution of theology and the church in a situation of radical change and pluriformity?

The first occasion for putting my thoughts and research results on such questions together in a more comprehensive manner came to me through Princeton Theological Seminary's unexpected invitation and honor to deliver the Stone Lectures in 2000. I gladly accepted this invitation and ventured to call the lecture series "The Postmodern Life Cycle." With this, the idea for the present book was born. Just like the Princeton lectures, this book is based on my work of twenty-five years of studying and researching the human life cycle with a special emphasis on religion in various stages of the life cycle—especially, religion in childhood, in adolescence, but also in adulthood.

The stimulus for writing this book came from the United States, and some of my studying and working on this topic also took place there, first at Harvard Divinity School and later at Princeton's Center of Theological Inquiry. At the same time, this book also clearly includes a European perspective in that I am teaching at the University of Tübingen in Germany. Maybe this kind of background may itself be considered somewhat postmodern. In any case, I take it to be expressive of a new international and dialogical practical theology that no longer limits itself to one particular national context. More and more, we are dealing with challenges that are not limited to one particular country or to one geographical context. Globalization is probably the clearest example for this, but postmodernity is no less an international phenomenon. So, I hope that my attempt to bring North American and European perspectives into dialogue with each other will prove to be helpful in deciphering the challenges of the postmodern life cycle.

Finally, this book has not been written for a strictly professional or narrow academic audience. While my considerations and analyses are based on academic research and not merely on personal impressions, I have tried to make my arguments as accessible as possible for readers outside the university and beyond the pastoral profession. In this sense, I am trying to follow the lead of a public theology that wants to make theological resources available to a broad audience by addressing issues of public concern. At the same time, I am deeply interested in making church and theology aware of the far-reaching challenges that the postmodern life cycle holds for their future work. This is also the reason for my attempt to develop consequences and practical perspectives for theology and the church throughout this book.

This book is dedicated to Princeton Theological Seminary and to its wonderful staff and students. Their questions and comments have been highly stimulating for my work on this project. In addition to this, I want to give special thanks to three American colleagues whose friendship has been of great value for my studies resulting in this book—Richard Osmer of Princeton Theological Seminary, Don S. Browning of the University of Chicago, and James W. Fowler of Emory University. Their publications have been of indispensable help for me and should be consulted by interested readers far beyond the various citations in my footnotes.[1] Without our joint efforts toward international cooperation in practical theology, this book would certainly not have been written.[2] Finally, I have to acknowledge that this book could also not have been written without the continuous support and encouragement of my wife, Marianne Martin. Should readers find the book readable or easy to understand, this would certainly be due to the critical questions that she, as the first reader, raised for me.

CHAPTER 1

The Religious Demands of Postmodern Life

Challenges for Practical Theology

When "postmodernity" came into the picture a little less than twenty years ago, it was often connected with Jean-François Lyotard's now famous prediction that all "master stories" had come to their end.[1] Interpreters of postmodernity tell us that all attempts at comprehensive description or explanation of society, history, human behavior, or the meaning of life have broken down. Postmodernity was and is seen as a time in which everything is becoming fluid and flexible, pluriform and contingent, fast and ephemeral.

Moreover, no schemes, let alone systems, seem to be available that could hold the increasing varieties of human experiences together. Everything appears to be a matter of which perspective one takes and in whose interest one prefers to speak. Postmodernity is a time of many stories and also of many different voices—the voices of different age groups, of women and men, of different ethnicities, to only mention a few of the many possible perspectives.

What kind of time is this for theology and the church? Is it a time for hopeful new beginnings, or is it a time of ever-increasing difficulties? Listening to ministers, teachers, counselors, Christian educators, and youth workers in the field, we learn of many worries and concerns. Is there still a place for Christian faith if there is no more room for master stories to guide our lives? How are children and youth to find any sense of direction if everything is pluriform

4

and contingent? What are the guidelines for responsible adulthood? Is it even possible for theology to communicate successfully with people whose lives have less and less in common?

Yet, there are others who happily embrace the advent of postmodernity, even among theologians, ministers, and educators. For them, postmodernity is not a threat to the Christian faith. Rather, in their understanding, postmodernity is opening up new possibilities for those who had been silenced and oppressed by the forces of modernity and who now, finally, dare to make themselves seen and heard—women, minorities, people without power. According to these observers, the end of all master stories does not exclude the possibility of Christian faith. Quite the opposite, the many stories that give expression to the Christian faith can only come to the fore where the master stories of modern science and economy have lost their uncontested dominance. In this view, postmodernity means liberation—liberation for the gospel and no less for the people who want to follow it by leading a Christian life and by shaping the communities in which they live.

So this is a time of hope and a time of doubt and despair—postmodernity has many faces. This book will not address all of them. There are too many aspects involved from the beginning. No single book can claim to cover them anymore. But it will be my attempt throughout this book to become clearer about what postmodernity actually means for theology and how theology and the church may respond to its challenges critically, as well as constructively, by making use of its potentials.

My focus will be on the life cycle—on the life cycle as it is changing with the advent of postmodernity. Yet fortunately or unfortunately, it is not at all clear how to define or to describe the postmodern life cycle. Some people even doubt that it makes sense to speak of a postmodern life cycle. So our first task is to get at least an initial understanding of what we mean by the "postmodern life cycle."

The Flexibility of the Human Life Cycle: Images of Family Life

In my teaching and lecturing, photographs of different family situations taken at different times during the twentieth century have often been helpful for gaining some understanding of how family life has changed. Such pictures typically capture different scenes from everyday life, from work as well as from leisure activities. In part, they remind us of our own childhood; in part, they refer us to the stories and descriptions that our parents and grandparents have told us. In any case, such pictorial material, which can be found in the photo albums of many families, makes intuitively clear that the human life cycle by no means is a constant or an anthropological given that would be exempt from change.

Pictures of this kind look different in different countries. Houses are different, cars are different, clothing is different, manners are different, and so forth. Yet what they all have in common is that they are clear indications of how much things have changed for the family during the last one hundred years.

Readers who have any doubts about this may want to consult their own family photo albums on their living room shelves. I myself very vividly recall three different scenes rendered in a German study on the modernization of childhood and the family.[2] The three scenes cover a span of sixty years. They come from the 1930s, the 1950s, and the 1990s:

The first scene shows a family in the 1930s. There are ten people in the picture, men and women, children and adults. They clearly belong to three different generations. Two things keep them busy together. They are taking a break from harvesting a field, and they are sharing a meal consisting of simple sandwiches and something to drink, which is poured from a simple pitcher.

The impression that this scene leaves on the observer is far from neutral. The whole situation is highly evocative, breathing peacefulness and also a certain gratitude. The people are enjoying each other. They may not be very rich, but they seem to have what they need. They are content.

The background of this picture is an agricultural society. Family life—here sharing a meal in the fields—is integrated with work. People are working together and they are eating together, and everything is happening more or less in the same place. There are no long-distance commutes. Three different generations are present on an everyday basis. Moreover, all of them are actively participating in the same task of working the fields.

The second scene in this study comes from the 1950s. In the center of the picture is a car, a small and simple car. While today such a vehicle might not even be able to trigger our nostalgia, the car in the picture clearly is more than a car. For many people and in many different countries, such a car was a powerful symbol indeed. It was the symbol of personal achievement and of individual mobility for everyone. But the car in the picture has even more implications for the family. The number of seats available in this vehicle tended to define the ideal size of the family: two adults and a maximum of two or three children—a limited family size that would also make it affordable to take a car vacation in the mountains or to the shore. And unless they had their own car, grandparents could not come along. It is no coincidence that the oldest generation is not present in this scene.

This kind of scene stands for the experience of improved living conditions in the decades after World War II. At that time the so-called nuclear family, which is limited to two generations (parents and children), was in the process of becoming the dominant form of family life. For many people, the home had ceased to be the workplace. Mobility included longer commutes, which again was made possible by the availability of cars.

With the third scene, we have arrived in the early 1990s, our immediate past or almost present. It shows how the promises of the 1950s have come to fruition in suburban life. The simple car of the 1950s has been replaced by a much more sophisticated vehicle, which is not only a means of transportation and not only a symbol of personal achievement. This car appears to be some kind of toy that testifies to the new affluence of many middle-class families at that time. The family does not have to go to the mountains anymore in order to enjoy life—it may do so in their own backyard, which might really be a close to perfect piece of lawn. And again, the family has become smaller. Paid work and family life are also clearly separate, but now this separation often applies to both parents. At best, there is one parent left to play with the children. The older generation of the grandparents is not visible anymore, not even in the home of the family. Probably they are living somewhere else, possibly far away. At least, they are not sharing their work and daily life with their children and grandchildren.

It is interesting to think about the question of what kind of scene from contemporary family life we ourselves would pick in order to capture our own situation. What kind of picture could convey the image of postmodernity? It is obviously easier to look back at former times and to realize how far away those times appear to us—the tranquility of agricultural society in the 1930s as well as the time of the 1950s or even the 1990s. So we may either wait for the future to give us a picture of who we were at the beginning of the new century, or readers may just insert their own observations and images of the postmodern life cycle. For the time being, it may be most appropriate to leave a question mark, which will remind us of the open question of how to picture the postmodern life cycle. At the end of this book, we will be in a better position to answer this question.

For now, it may be helpful to imagine what the different kinds of family experience mean for an individual person on his or her passage through the life cycle. The first scene points to a life cycle that is very much predefined from birth. In most cases, the person moves along through life by taking over the positions that other members of the family had filled—the position of mother or father, of field hand, of working in the house, and so forth. The family with its sequence of generations defined much of one's life. There were few choices to be made about this. One's future looked like the family's past. In industrial societies this continuity between past and future comes under attack. To move through the life cycle now means to strive for achievements that, if possible, will allow the person to surpass his (and sometimes her) parents. There are achievements of education and training, and they are measured by the success of a working life defined by status and income. Choices are becoming more important for the individual, but, for the most part, they are choices between clearly defined alternatives like different kinds of education or work. Probably it is at this point that the experience of an individual person moving through the life cycle today has become most different. Choices have multiplied, and they are no longer predefined. Nor is it clear what the consequences of such choices will be in the long run. The past of one's family does not offer much direction for the future anymore, and society holds no more promises of clear-cut professional futures.

Let me return to my earlier question concerning a preliminary understanding of the difference between the modern and the postmodern life cycle. What do the pictures or scenes from family life tell us about the life cycle? Three aspects seem especially important.

(1) First, it is obvious how much the shape of daily life has changed over the generations of the last fifty or sixty years. The routines in which everyday life is embedded have changed in almost every respect, even within the family. Fewer persons are involved. The character of family life has been strongly affected by moving paid work away from the home and by relocating it in separate institutions

of industry or trade. Consequently, the temporal order of daily life also had to change. In all these respects, the life cycle has been subject to radical changes. To put it into more general terms, the life cycle is not an anthropological given that can never change. Our contemporary situation makes us aware of how flexible the life cycle really is or, at least, how flexible it has become.

It is helpful to think about the life cycle in terms of a threefold distinction between the *premodern*, the *modern*, and the *postmodern* experience. In a traditional agricultural situation, individual life is built into an integrated pattern of living and working together of three or more generations. Consequently, the individual person proceeds more or less naturally and automatically through a life cycle that is, for the most part, predetermined by one's birth into a certain family. By looking at their parents and grandparents, children are able to tell what their own life will be like once they reach the respective age. As pointed out above, there is much continuity between past and future. Given the preindustrial background of this kind of life and society, I call this the *premodern life cycle*.

The designation "premodern" is, of course, not very exact. Taken literally, it means everything "before modernity," which applies to everything from the Stone Age to the medieval period. It would certainly be misleading to assume that the human life cycle has stayed the same through all these different times. When I speak of the "premodern life cycle," my claim is a different one. I do not want to make romantic assumptions about life in earlier periods of history or the former stability of the life cycle. I am interested in a backdrop against which the contemporary changes of the life cycle can be discerned. So let us look further. What happens to the life cycle once agricultural society is on the wane?

Even without considering any details, one thing is obvious. With the expanding influence of industrialization and of paid labor outside the family, the life cycle turns into a much more demanding task for the individual. Not only does family life become separated from work while families become smaller and less stable, the life cycle itself is redefined as a career–a career that for the most part is measured by the economic and social success achieved by the respective individual. In this sense, increasing success and personal achievement are the characteristic ideals of the *modern life cycle*.[3]

Again, it must be admitted that the designation as "career" is a very preliminary way of describing the modern life cycle, and, as I want to show in the subsequent chapters, it is also a very one-sided, contradictory, or even ideological way of viewing the life cycle. Yet there can be no doubt about the central influence that the idea of making a career, or of having missed one's opportunity for a successful career, has had on modern life. In this view, the family into which a child is born should not determine the course of his or her life cycle. The model of one's parents and grandparents no longer is the mold for one's own future life. Modern society holds the promise of many opportunities for everyone who is able to make use of them.

Toward the end of the twentieth century, new developments have come into view that are still hard to characterize. Some observers speak of a new type of biography in the sense that life has turned into an individual project and into a matter of personal choice.[4] Others are more skeptical about whether a postmodern life cycle really exists or if we are just witnessing a further extension of modernity.[5] At this early point of my analysis, I prefer to keep this question open. Suffice it to say, at this initial stage, that the *postmodern life cycle* must be what comes after the model of the life cycle as career has lost at least some of its power and persuasiveness. This preliminary understanding will be enough to get us started with further investigations into the changes that we are currently observing.

(2) Let me make a second point about the different scenes of family life rendered above. The pictures on which I have based my descriptions are not simply pictures of reality. This is true even though they are photographs. Photographs of the family as they are found in family albums tend to be highly artificial and symbolic. Often, they are not just snapshots taken by chance, and, in any case, they are not the result of realistic documentation. In earlier times, such pictures were often taken only after a lengthy procedure of arranging and rearranging the people in the picture, always attending to the questions of who should be in the picture and in front of what background, with what additional objects like houses, cars, trees, mountains, and so forth. And certainly, not every picture was allowed a place in the album or behind a frame.

This is why such pictures are not to be confused with the *reality* of family life. Rather, these pictures are trying to capture certain *ideals*– ideals of what the family should be, in the eyes of the photographer or according to the views of those who hold on to these pictures.

Consequently, the scenes of family life rendered above are not really documentary. They are not indicative of what the family really was twenty, thirty, or fifty years ago. But they can tell us something about what the family was supposed to be at that time, at least within the traditional middle class. The ideal character of such pictures and scenes also explains why certain realities of family life are absent from the official photographs. This is most obvious for the situation in the late twentieth century. The suburban family enjoying life is only one side. The other side is, for example, the situation of a single mother who is trying to finish her education while holding her baby on her lap. Most likely this woman is lacking the resources to fully participate in the world of material enjoyments, and her tight schedule does not give her much leeway for playing with the toys of postmodern life.

So there is the *ideal* and there are the many *realities of life*. And obviously, the ideal and the real do not coincide. Yet it is easy to see that the ideal life cycle is not only different from the real life cycle, but that the ideal model also has its effects on the reality of the life cycle—by guiding public opinion, by forming personal aspirations, by shaping policies, and by suppressing those phenomena that do not fit the ideal. For this reason, it is important not only to study the life cycle empirically but also to include the ideal models and renderings of this life cycle. This is why the present study will put a strong emphasis on the ideas and ideals that are connected to the life cycle in contemporary culture.

The inclusion of ideal models and their relationship to the realities of the life cycle is further motivated by the focus on postmodernity. According to some observers, postmodernity especially affects such models or ideas: If postmodernity means, for example, the end of all clear-cut models of the family—some sociologists even speak of the "postfamilial family"[6]—does this also mean the end of all singular models of the life cycle? Does it even make sense to speak of a "cycle" anymore when everything is just in flux—moving back and forth, sideways as well as up and down, but never completing an ideal circular shape or gestalt? This will be another central question to be addressed in the present study.

(3) The third aspect that I want to bring to the reader's attention with the scenes of family life described above has often been overlooked in the discussions about the life cycle. The scenes of family life have not only an ideal and therefore symbolic nature, but they also clearly include a *religious dimension*. They indicate or even prescribe how individual life is to become whole, how it is to achieve a perfect and complete shape. They are images of how life can become meaningful. With this observation, we have arrived at the point where *theology* must enter the picture. Theological analysis is needed in order to come to terms with the images of a meaningful life, not only in terms of acquiring a certain faith but also in terms of evaluating the ideal images of life offered, for example, by the media. Many people

have come to realize, in the different contexts of their life and work, that the images of the meaningful life cycle are not always as harmless as they appear to be at first glance. On the contrary, ideal images of human life have always produced victims—by devaluing all those whose lives do not conform to the ideal image and whose lives are then bereft of meaning and value. And this is even more true once the meaning given to the life cycle is of an ultimate or religious nature. In this case, the lack of meaning will also be ultimate. So the religious dimension of the life cycle is of special importance and deserves special attention, not only for theologians but for everyone who is interested in the experiences connected to the life cycle.

Moreover, it is easy to see why changes in the life cycle inherently are—or at least should be—a topic for Christian theology. In many cases, such changes not only concern the levels of daily routine but they also affect the structures of meaning that are connected to the life cycle—the images of wholeness and completion. At this point, I want to mention a few questions in order to illustrate how a theological perspective can enter the process of interpreting different experiences of the life cycle: How, for example, do the images of wholeness and completion that are operative in society relate to a theological understanding of wholeness and completion? Do these images allow the human beings to be truly human, or do they lead us into the temptations of self-deification and paralysis? Which images or ideals are helpful and healthy; which ones are not? How can we avoid being lured by empty promises and into directions that turn out to be dead ends?

Such questions indicate that theology may have a public role to play in dealing with the postmodern life cycle, a role that, in any case, is important to culture and society in general. Yet whoever wants to make reference to Christian theology in a postmodern situation must also face the challenges of the postmodern religious situation. Many analysts assume that postmodernity affects religion no less than it affects individual life. Therefore, we must now turn to the situation of religion in postmodernity.

Some Features of Contemporary Religious Life

It has often been noted that contemporary religious life, first of all, has turned out to be different than the prophets of modernity had expected. Not too long ago, many observers, be they social scientists or theologians, saw religion as being on the wane, giving way more and more to a powerful and comprehensive process of secularization.

It was expected that religious worldviews would increasingly be replaced by scientific and rational views of the world and that personal religious convictions would be allowed to exert only a minimal influence on one's life.

In the United States, two books by the Harvard theologian Harvey Cox can stand symbolically for the changing expectations. In 1965, Cox published his best-selling book on the *Secular City,* in which he describes the impact of secular urban life and foresees a future without religion.[7] Roughly twenty years later, in 1984, he published his sequel, *Religion in the Secular City,* in which he observes the unexpected return of religion to what he formerly called the secular city.[8] In this latter book, Cox points to vital new forms of religion that have entered the picture after the 1960s, like fundamentalism on the one hand and liberation theology on the other. From this perspective, religion is as alive as ever, even if it looks different from the past. At the same time, his book gives evidence to the shaky nature of all earlier prophecies of the end of religion, which turned out to be less empirical than speculative and without real basis. And finally, he raises the question of what a postmodern theology could look like, thus pioneering, in his field, the question that I am posing in respect to the life cycle.

The expected decline of religion has not become a reality, not in the United States and also not in many other parts of the world, even though parts of Europe and especially the former East Block countries in Europe and Asia definitively are a special case.[9] Yet, although the end of religion seems to be much further away than secularization theory had expected, things clearly have changed. For the most part, the traditional churches in the Western world have lost many of their members, and, possibly even more important, they have lost what sociologists call their monopoly on religion in society.[10] If, thirty or forty years ago, to be religious meant, at least for the majority, to be a member of a mainline church, the situation has changed markedly in this respect. On the one hand, there is a growing number of so-called unchurched people who do not claim any affiliation with a religious denomination or group. On the other hand, there is the increasing influence of smaller Christian denominations and groups as well as of non-Christian religions that have acquired an increasing presence in many Western countries.[11]

This situation is aptly described by a number of terms that refer to different aspects of the contemporary religious situation. Since these terms will come up again and again in the following chapters, it seems helpful to state briefly my understanding of them here.

- *Pluralization* refers to the process through which religious orientations and attitudes have taken on a multiple shape. This includes the inner pluralism of Christianity, of different groups and denominations and subgroups within the denominations, as well as the religious plurality of a multireligious society comprising a number of different religions beyond Christianity.

- Religious *individualization* is the flip side of religious pluralization. It means that religious orientations are less and less determined by churches or religious institutions and by the traditions for which these institutions stand. Rather, religion becomes a matter of individual choice—an inescapable consequence of a situation in which the presence of different religious possibilities is experienced from childhood on. In a well-known book, the sociologist Peter Berger speaks of the "heretical imperative" in order to characterize the situation of forced religious choice for each and everyone in society.[12] Similarly, the now current term *spirituality* conveys a personal religious interest that is not connected to religious institutions, formal membership, traditional authorities, and so forth. Spirituality, in this context, often means a type of religion that can be Christian in the sense of an individualized Christianity that is not related to any congregation.

- Often a third term is used to describe our contemporary religious situation: the *privatization* of religion. In this context, privatization means that religion has become a private affair.[13] This understanding includes several aspects. In part, privatization refers to the emergence of a private sphere in modernity—a sphere that is separate from work, economy, and politics. And it may also refer to the legal separation between state and church or between state and religion. In either case, so the argument runs, religion is relegated and confined to the private realm. According to this view, modern and postmodern religion is a matter only of personal life—a matter of intimate character that rarely is talked about in public and sometimes is not even a topic of conversation in the family.

Observations concerning the increasingly intimate character of religion should definitely be taken seriously. Yet at the same time, contemporary social analysts like José Casanova and, in part, Peter Beyer have pointed out the public role that religion has played, and continues to play, in many countries at the beginning of the twenty-first century.[14] Not only is there a Religious Right in the United States, and not only are there religiously motivated political movements for peace, justice, and the integrity of the creation in many countries of the Western world, there is also the Muslim influence on politics in many Arab and Asian countries. So the contemporary situation has turned religion into a private matter, but it also includes countermovements of religion reclaiming a public role for itself–a process that is not without its specific conflicts, as becomes clear when we take up a fourth term: *globalization.*

- In the context of religion, *globalization* has come into the picture only recently. For some people it may still be surprising that globalization is even mentioned in the context of our religious situation. All around the world, globalization is understood as an economic process with implications for finances and technology. But does globalization also have religious implications? One of the most well-known statements on globalization and religion comes from Samuel Huntington.[15] For Huntington, globalization includes the danger of a "clash of civilizations," which really is a clash of the different cultures and religions of the world in that culture and religion are an integral part of the different civilizations. With globalization bringing these religions closer together geographically, there also is a growing potential for conflict and religious hostility. Other observers like Roland Robertson, Peter Beyer, and Anthony Giddens also speak of religious implications of globalization.[16] According to them, many of the tendencies mentioned above, most of all pluralization and individualization, receive additional strength and backing from globalization. In this view, the emergence of a new consciousness of the world as a single place adds a whole new background to our religious outlooks, possibly relativizing them and, in any case, challenging them with the awareness of the many religious possibilities available in this world. This is why there is a close relationship between postmodernity and globalization.

Of course, this reference to the concepts of religious pluralization, individualization, privatization, and of the emergent process of globalization is not much more than offering readers a panoramic picture with a few very broad strokes. Yet the main task in this introductory chapter is not to produce a detailed picture of postmodern religion as it has been described by sociologists of religion.[17] Rather, my focus is on the postmodern *life cycle* and on the religious dimensions that this life cycle entails. Therefore, the question must be how the contemporary religious situation affects the life cycle. To put it differently: What are the religious demands of postmodern life regarding the life cycle?

In looking at the different scenes of family life, we hit upon the problematic effects of ideal images of wholeness and completion that are offered as descriptions of the successful life cycle. And we have also come to realize that such ideals often are religious ideals bestowing the life cycle with ultimate meaning and value or, conversely, denying such meaning and value to a particular life. Having at least briefly taken account of the situation of postmodern religion, we are now in a position to attempt a first summary of what may be considered the specific demands and challenges of the postmodern life cycle. Three interrelated demands are of special importance.

- The first of these demands obviously arises from *changes in the life cycle itself.* As we have seen, the life cycle is losing its traditional shape and structure. The trajectories of individual life are becoming more and more pluriform. Life itself has become a project for which everyone is responsible by himself or herself. In a wide sense, this project may be called religious in that it always hinges upon the ultimate meaning and value by which the life cycle is guided or judged, in the eyes of the individual person as well as in those of others. This is the *challenge of the life cycle under reconstruction.*

- Second, the *religious meaning and values* available for guiding and supporting the project of the postmodern life cycle have also taken on a *pluriform* shape. No longer is there a clear and unanimous source from which the individual person can gain religious insight and faith. Rather, there is religious plurality, in the church as well as beyond the church. To find and to personally adopt a religious faith has also become a project in the sense that the individual person has to chose from many different options that are present from childhood on and that claim to be equally valid. So if the postmodern life cycle contains the potential of a new and intensified search for ultimate meaning, it is a postmodern religion that is encountered by this search. If the human life cycle has come into flux, so also has postmodern religion. This is the *challenge of finding and adopting a faith* in a religiously plural situation.

- Third, finding a faith of one's own as the foundation on which to build a life cycle is not only a task for childhood or adolescence. Having been nurtured and raised in a certain faith or religion will not necessarily solve the issue in postmodern adulthood. Rather, finding a faith becomes a *lifelong project*. The demands of the postmodern life cycle remain present, challenging us ever anew: What does it mean to live a Christian life in a society that constantly conveys that such a life is only one of many different possible options? And how do I make sense of my faith when I am aware of all the different options? This is the *challenge of maintaining a faith* vis-à-vis many options.

Putting it all together in one phrase, the challenge is how to come to terms with a life cycle that presents itself like a permanent construction site, with an overabundance of competing construction plans and with no clear criteria for choosing among them.

In concluding this section, let me also point out that these challenges and demands of the postmodern life cycle have far-reaching implications not only for the individual person but also for church and society. In connection with religious pluralization, individualization, and globalization, we hit upon the growing fear of a "clash of civilizations" as Huntington has called it. An increasingly multireligious situation can easily breed intolerance, religious conflict, and even extreme violence. To this, we should add the danger of society's losing its normative basis. The less there is a common religion that may hold society together, the more difficult it becomes to conceive of a common culture and of common values. No doubt, religious diversity came into the picture long ago. It was a hallmark of modern Western society, long before postmodernity had come about. Yet religious pluralization and individualization may still be more than the familiar religious diversity that in a Western context was often really some kind of Christian diversity in that the different churches, denominations, and groups still wanted to be Christian, even if in different ways. This is no longer the case. Today's religious diversity goes far beyond Christianity. It includes non-Christian religions as well as nonreligious worldviews. Consequently, finding a shared basis for common values has become increasingly difficult.

Finally, turning to the church, the postmodern life cycle also holds important challenges. The traditional churches especially seem to be faced with enormous difficulties of staying in touch with the lives of those living in postmodernity. Maybe it would be even more accurate to say that the real difficulty lies in how postmodern individuals may become convinced that staying affiliated with a religious institution is still worthwhile. What exactly is the meaning of the gospel vis-à-vis the many other religious and nonreligious convictions that have become available? Is there any reason to prefer the Christian tradition over others? And what does this tradition mean for the life cycle–the postmodern life cycle as it is experienced and shaped today? Unless the church is able to find viable and convincing answers to such questions, its future is quite uncertain.

Obviously, the postmodern life cycle holds many challenges–challenges for the church, for society, and for the individual person. How are we to deal with these challenges? Let me conclude this introductory chapter with some comments on the procedure that I want to pursue in the following chapters and on what the reader may expect from the analyses in this book.

Two Ways of Approaching Postmodernity

There are many different ways in which the topic of postmodernity can be approached. Philosophers and social analysts speak of postmodernity, and so do journalists, politicians, economists, and many others.[18] My own perspective is theological; or, to be more precise, it is focused on practical theology. And since this perspective is in need of explanation, it seems helpful to introduce readers in this introduction not only to the kind of questions that I will take up in the following chapters, but to also include some initial remarks on how I want to address these questions. In other words, I will be using a specific approach or methodology, which must be introduced to the readers.

Without making this explicit so far, I have already made use of this approach or methodology. Especially in the section on changes of family life, I was trying to begin with the actual experience of contemporary people, including their memories and their impressions, for example, from family albums and from the photographs collected in them. Sometimes this kind of procedure–taking today's experiences and situations as a starting point–is considered the methodology of practical theology. It may be called a *methodology from below*.

Such a methodology from below does not approach postmodernity in terms of philosophical concepts and definitions. It does not take a conceptual comparison between premodernity, modernity, and postmodernity as its starting point in order to then apply such concepts deductively to the praxis of social and Christian life. According to a widespread assumption, a deductive approach or *methodology from above* would be closer to philosophical or systematic theology.[19] The strength of the deductive approach is conceptual clarity; its weakness is its relatively abstract character, which can imply distance to contemporary experience and to the praxis of the church. For the inductive approach of practical theology, the opposite can be said. It is close to today's world and to the praxis of the church, but it may be lacking conceptual clarity. Contemporary experiences and situations are often opaque, multifaceted, and, in any case, ambivalent.

So there are potential dangers and shortcomings in either approach. Therefore, practical theology should not be identified with a methodology from below, at least not in a naïve sense of only looking at experiences and situations without making use of theoretical frameworks or concepts. Rather, in my understanding, practical theology must indeed take the experience of today's people as seriously as possible. At the same time, this experience may not even be understood if we do not have eyes to see and ears to hear—or, speaking less metaphorically, if we do not have theories, concepts, and categories that enable us to make sense of what contemporary people tell us. To make sense of something always implies becoming aware of differences and making distinctions. Otherwise, everything will just look the same. This is why practical theology is in need of concepts and categories as much as any other theoretical approach.

Take the scenes of family life rendered above as an example: In order to make sense of what these scenes and situations contain, I soon had to apply concepts of different historical times, and I had to become clear about what is real in them rather than ideal or even religious. So working from experience also requires conceptual tools and theoretical clarity. The approach of practical theology cannot be based on making do without conceptual distinctions. What makes it different from most approaches in systematic theology or philosophy, however, is its continuous and intentional attempt to stay close to people's experiences. Addressing the life cycle is a good example of this procedure. An analysis of the postmodern life cycle that does justice to the criteria of practical theology can only be developed in close contact and dialogue with contemporary experiences, which is not always the case with corresponding analyses from systematic theology.[20] But such an analysis also includes the tasks of working with different models of the life cycle and of evaluating these models.

However, this is still a very general statement. Beyond such reflections on methodology and practical theology in general, we have to be aware of the special nature of our topic—the postmodern life cycle. Clearly, the choice of a certain methodology must be in accordance with the subject we want to address. In a preliminary way, we may say that it is characteristic of the postmodern situation that, by its very nature, this situation escapes all clear-cut conceptual frameworks. As it is repeated over and over again in the literature, there is no consensual definition of postmodernity,[21] at least not so far, and possibly there will never be one since the character of postmodernity contradicts the intention of such definitions. If this is true, the way in which the postmodern life cycle is addressed must be reflective of this situation. It must take the fluid character of postmodernity seriously, not only as a specific topic or content but also in terms of the methods used in approaching this topic. What does this mean for the analysis in the chapters to follow?

Since we cannot presuppose what is meant by the postmodern life cycle, we have to make sure that we will at least be able to find out what it is. And since we have a special interest in the experience of contemporary people as well as in the praxis of the church, we must have a constant eye on including these perspectives as much as possible. In the light of these needs, I have arranged the five chapters that make up the body of this book as probes of five stages or sections of the life cycle: childhood, youth, postadolescence, adulthood, and old age.

When I lecture on these topics, people sometimes raise the question of whether these different ages even still exist in postmodernity and if these traditional designations still make sense. I think this question is very much to the point. If we want to become clear about the postmodern life cycle, we will be better off not presupposing any of the traditional understandings. And this is exactly what I mean by calling the chapters below my "probes." I will not presuppose that these ages still exist or that they have only changed in content. Instead, I want to use them as test cases in order to find out how the traditional understandings and views of these ages have been affected by postmodernity.

It is for this reason that I have chosen a certain format to use in these chapters. In each case, I will start by asking, with respect to one particular segment of the life cycle, (1) about its once *modern understanding,* which now has become the traditional understanding. In a further step, I will ask (2) about the *changes* that may be observed when we compare this "modern" life cycle with today's experience in childhood, adolescence, adulthood, and old age. Readers may have noticed that I have just left out postadolescence, which I mention above as one of my test cases. The reason for not mentioning postadolescence here has to do with the special nature of this age. This period of the life cycle does not exist in the modern understanding. The classic view sees people moving from adolescence into adulthood, with nothing else between these two ages than a short and more or less successful transition. So postadolescence needs a different approach that is in line with the special nature of this age. Throughout all chapters, and with respect to the modern life cycle as well as with today's situation, my emphasis will be (3) on the challenges for religion in general and, more specifically, for the Christian faith. Based on these chapters, we will also be in the position to ask, in a third step within each chapter, how *theology* and the *church* may respond critically and constructively to the challenges posed by the postmodern situation. In all of this, I will try to avoid all nostalgia for the past but also the naïve optimism that confuses postmodernism with paradise. The hermeneutics of suspicion will be applied to both, to modernity as well as to postmodernity.

My three-step procedure obviously depends on a comparison between the modern and the postmodern life cycle. For this comparison, I will draw upon one of the most influential models of the life cycle—the model of Erik H. Erikson. Erikson developed his model in various publications beginning in the 1950s.[22] It became influential in many fields within the social sciences but also in practical theology. Comparing Erikson's model with today's experiences is therefore of special interest, not only in terms of testing out the contemporary usefulness of this model but also for examining its meaning and use in practical theology.

I will draw upon Erikson's model mostly as a backdrop for comparisons between the modern (now traditional) life cycle on the one hand and the postmodern life cycle on the other. So this is not a book on Erikson.[23] But the following chapters can be read as a commentary on some of his ideas from today's perspective.

According to the plan of this book, chapters 2 and 3 as well as chapters 5 and 6 will roughly follow the same procedure of looking at one segment of the life cycle by sequentially using three different lenses: *modernity, postmodernity, responses of church and theology.* This implies that there will be a strong emphasis on the empirical description of today's experiences, and this will include constant reference to the social sciences. Chapter 4 deals with postadolescence as a new stage of the life cycle. The last chapter (chapter 7), however, will be different. It will bring into focus another question that I consider decisive in our grappling with postmodernity—the question of a theology of the life cycle.

Asking about a theology of the life cycle implies that, in the last chapter, we change our perspective. If the bulk of this book takes our contemporary situation as the starting point and views theology and the church in a responding role (although never only by adaptation, but always critically and constructively), the last chapter will try out an alternative approach. Here, theological perspectives will be used as challenges for the contemporary situation, thus making explicit what is true implicitly for all of my considerations. I am not advocating an adaptive theology that sees its main task to be current, fashionable, or attractive to those living in postmodernity. Rather, even in making the contemporary situation the starting point, I am inviting readers to be involved in a critical evaluation of this situation including its religious and theological implications and also including the critical potential that is inherent to the Christian tradition.

This brings us to a last point that must be mentioned in this introductory chapter. The study of the postmodern life cycle and of its religious implications is necessarily an interdisciplinary endeavor. It must bring into dialogue different academic disciplines: psychology, philosophy, sociology, and theology, to only mention the most important ones. This kind of dialogue is another characteristic of practical theology as I understand it. And it is also a task that is especially important today because so many students of the human life cycle show no interest in religion. One example of this neglect is the otherwise brilliant study *In Over Our Heads: The Mental Demands of Modern Life* by Robert Kegan, which does not include religion among the demands studied.[24] When I called this introductory chapter *Religious Demands of Postmodern Life,* I actually had in mind the need to start a critical and constructive dialogue with such authors and to complete their accounts of modern and postmodern life. My whole book can be read as an attempt to open this dialogue.

CHAPTER 2

Born into a Plural World

Growing Up between Multicultural Richness and Religious Homelessness

Numerous accounts of childhood and of childhood religion have been published over the last decades.[1] The changing shape of childhood is of special concern for parents and educators as well as for all those who are worried about the future of Western culture and societies. Philosophers of education have pointed out the special value of childhood for education and learning of all kinds. Psychologists have offered their insights on how childhood becomes, for better or worse, the destiny for many or most people in adulthood. Theologians and pastoral counselors have had to learn how to listen for the hidden impact of childhood experiences on the religious life of adults. Currently, media researchers are cautioning the public that what used to be known as "childhood" is actually under siege by the still growing influence of an increasing number of media that are making their way into the child's home. It is no surprise that Neil Postman's book on *The Disappearance of Childhood* has become an international bestseller.[2] Parents, educators, and theologians alike are highly concerned about the future of childhood.

There are many reasons to be interested in what being a child means today and how the contemporary experience of childhood influences the religious life of children. The present chapter, however, is not just another consideration of such general observations or worries. Rather, it follows the specific interest in the postmodern life cycle that is the key question of this book. Moreover, this chapter is concerned with viewing the postmodern life cycle from the perspective of practical theology. Before further addressing childhood as the main topic in this chapter, it may be helpful to outline this special interest in some more detail.

In the first chapter of this book, we have seen that the human life cycle is under reconstruction and that the religious dimensions of the life cycle are strongly influenced by the changing shape of contemporary life. The questions of the postmodern life cycle and of its meaning for church and theology must be approached through the lens of contemporary experiences of those who are moving through this life cycle or, to be more open, through whatever has become of the life cycle in a postmodern world. And since the present study, as pointed out above, is not to approach postmodernity by taking the philosophical or theological debate as its starting point but with a strong focus on the changes within the life cycle itself, we must now proceed to an exploration of the various stages of the life cycle. In doing this, we follow a chronological order, beginning with childhood and ending with old age. At the same time, the traditional shape of this order cannot be presupposed naïvely anymore. It is no longer to be taken for granted that chronological age is the one main characteristic that allows for a basic orientation. Lifestyles or social and cultural backgrounds as well as individual circumstances may tell us more about a person than his or her age.

The main reason for working our way through the life cycle from childhood to old age has to do with the comparisons in which the present explorations are interested. By taking the modern life cycle (which now, from the perspective of postmodernity, is the traditional life cycle) as our starting point, we can compare its "classic" descriptions with contemporary observations. As pointed out above, I will specifically make use of the work of Erik H. Erikson as a backdrop for this kind of comparison, thus using him as the major representative of the traditional or classic view of the modern life cycle. In other words, the breakdown of this book along the chronological order of the modern life cycle is not a tacit affirmation of traditional views of the life cycle. Rather, it is expected to allow for maximum contrast by examining, for each major stage of life, if and how things have actually changed from modernity to postmodernity.

Following the procedure of approaching postmodernity from an inductive point of view, I will start out by contrasting the traditional modern understanding of childhood with the challenges of today's experience of childhood. One of these challenges–the experience of religious diversity or plurality–will be given special attention because it is often connected to postmodernity and because it entails far-reaching consequences for childhood religion and for religious education. The discussion of this experience will be focused on the tension between multicultural openness on the one hand and religious belonging on the other.

The Modern View: Childhood as the Basis for Religious Belonging

At first glance, it may be surprising to call understanding childhood as the basis for religious belonging a *modern* view. Is there anything modern about this understanding of childhood as the time when people first acquire a religious faith and when they have to learn the stories and teachings of a certain religion? It almost seems to be a natural given that children have to be introduced to a faith and that this introduction should go along with the expectation that they will stay with this faith, be it as children or be it as adolescents and adults.

In order to become somewhat clearer about the specifically modern understanding of religion in childhood, we have to have a closer look at what understandings may be found before modernity and how these understandings changed with modernity. Some considerations of premodern times prove to be helpful.

The importance of religious education in childhood has, in fact, been emphasized throughout history. Even in antiquity and in the Middle Ages, educators often referred to the "waxen" or "wax-like" character of the child, which was considered to be especially open and suitable for Christian nurture and for catechetical instruction. The basic idea was to begin early so that the unique time of childhood with its openness for religious education would not be missed. It is much easier, says Martin Luther for example, to work with those "little young trees" than with the "dry wood," as he metaphorically identified the character of adults.[3] Luther's view is not only expressive of his theological perception of the increasing effects of sin over the course of life, it is also expressive of the medieval awareness of the flexibility of children's character that makes early education a promising enterprise.

So in a sense, it is certainly true that religious education in childhood has always been considered natural and important, and there is nothing exclusively modern about this idea. It is interesting to note, however, that, about two hundred years ago, modern philosophers of education such as Johann Heinrich Pestalozzi or theologians and religious educators such as Friedrich Schleiermacher took this view of religion in childhood one important step farther, thus giving it a new and specifically modern turn. These early modern interpreters introduced the understanding that there is a special psychological basis for religious education in childhood that has to do with the early experiences of children. They assumed that the relationship to God builds, and in fact must build, on an earlier experience of human relationships that produce the psychological basis for faith in God.[4] According to this view, the relationship to God must always be grounded in the early relationship to mother and father in childhood. Consequently, it is here, at the very beginning of the life cycle, that the idea of God as well as hope in God must take hold. "God is the God of my mother," says Pestalozzi in a famous quotation: "He is the God of my heart, he is the God of her heart. I know no other God, the God of my brain is a fancy."[5] Or, to use Schleiermacher's words, the child's "love for the mother" is the "first seed" of religion.[6] Both Pestalozzi and Schleiermacher thus give a new religious meaning to childhood. For them, childhood is much more than a time that is especially open for educational influences. Rather, childhood actually includes and furnishes the experiental and psychological basis that is necessary to start the process of religious development and education. Childhood has become the foundation of religion, the indispensable basis for all religion in later life.

Calling this psychological interpretation of the beginnings of religious development and education a modern view can be justified by pointing out the dual focus on human experience and on the human person rather than on revelation and on objective teachings. This focus is typically modern. Yet, it should not be overlooked that religious educators such as Pestalozzi and Schleiermacher were by no means naïve advocates of modernity. Quite the opposite: At the time, they wanted to defend religious education and the child against the modern reductionism of a rationalist and utilitarian education. Their reference to the psychological origins of faith and religion in childhood was meant to exactly do this: Give an anthropological meaning to the religious dimension within the experiences of children and also within education. They wanted to defend this dimension against those who only aimed at increasing the rational abilities of children. This intention gives their philosophies of education a critical thrust beyond the narrow rationalism of modernity. Yet at least from today's retrospective point of view, this defense against modernism still included a strong modernist tendency itself. Their view of childhood religion was itself in danger of a reductionist interpretation, for example, by reducing religion to feelings or to childhood relationships with the mother.

Not surprisingly, this understanding of the psychological presuppositions of religion in childhood is not the only one that modernity has produced. As I just mentioned in describing the backdrop against which Pestalozzi and Schleiermacher set forth their ideas, modernity's general emphasis on rationality also included a strong critique and scornful rejection of all childhood religion as childish and as a lasting detriment to human reason. Jean-Jacques Rousseau, for example, advised against any attempt at religious education during childhood.[7] He was convinced that religion had no legitimate place in the life cycle before adolescence, among other reasons because he thought children lacked the mental capacities even for understanding the meaning of the Christian faith, let alone for personally adopting it. This is why Rousseau suggested deferring religious education until the age of fourteen.

While a one-sided emphasis on rationality and a corresponding skepticism about the religion of children remained influential in modern education throughout most of modernity, the competing intention of identifying the psychological basis of faith in childhood has also received considerable attention. In twentieth-century psychology, the idea of the psychological presuppositions for faith in God were taken up by modern psychologists and especially by psychoanalysts. Sigmund Freud himself, the founder of the psychoanalytic movement, belonged more on the side of the modern critics of religion.[8] His focus was on the neuroticizing influence of religion in childhood, especially during the years when the superego or conscience develops. So while Freud was not convinced of the healthy influence of religion in general and while he did not foresee a constitutive role for childhood religion in a positive sense, he was still convinced that the religious experiences during childhood are decisive for later life.

It was one of the most influential psychologists and psychoanalysts of the twentieth century who, through his work on the human life cycle, gave the idea of the positive role of childhood religion new meaning and importance. This psychologist was, of course, Erik Erikson, who described the corresponding psychological processes in terms of basic trust, of childhood identification, and of the family as the first basis of group identity.[9] According to his account of psychosocial development during childhood, the trustworthy relationship between mother and infant is the origin of religious longing and hope. It is in the mother's face that the infant comes to know herself, and that face becomes the precursor of God's face. Erikson describes this process in almost poetic ways. In his *Young Man Luther* we find the following passage:

> ...only religion restores the earliest sense of appeal to a Provider, a Providence. In the Judaeo-Christian tradition, no prayer indicates this more clearly than "The Lord make His Face to shine upon you and be gracious unto you. The Lord shift up His countenance upon you and give you peace"; and no prayerful attitude better than the uplifted face, hopeful of being recognized.[10]

As the child gradually grows older, it is the firm identification with the parents that carries this psychosocial process of religious development further. This identification connects the religious experience of early childhood with the religious education by mother, father, and the extended family. The religious dimension, included implicitly by the experience of "basic trust" (or "mistrust"), now becomes explicit, and it is still mediated through the relationships within the family.

The experience of being firmly rooted as a child in the faith of one's parents has been praised, for example, by the French author Jacques Lusseyran in the 1960s. In his autobiographical writings, he speaks of the "feeling of warmth" and of the intimate "protection" that was for him the "beginning of faith," never giving way to "metaphysical doubt."[11] And even a contemporary author such as New York journalist and mother Martha Fay speaks no less vividly of the experience "that one's self, wrapped in the tender batting of one's perfect family, inhabits the true center of the universe, all its ways the right ways, all its customs eternal."[12] Such reports are one of the main reasons why many people want their children to grow up exactly like this—firmly rooted in the faith of their parents and with a clear sense of belonging to a particular Christian congregation and religious community. So in the modern view, the early stages of the life cycle are considered as the seedbed of personal faith and also as the firm basis of religious group identity in the sense of belonging to one's parents and, through them, to the one true religion.

This view is still very attractive, at least to many parents and religious educators. Yet the praise of religious grounding in childhood has not always been unanimous. Ever since modern educators such as Rousseau or critical psychoanalysts such as Freud entered the picture, there has been the concern that early religious education will, in fact, overpower the child. Again and again, religious education in childhood has been challenged and criticized because, in this critical perspective, it is actually forcing a moral and religious scheme on the children. The child is seen as vulnerable and as defenseless against religious indoctrination that, according to the critics, can only harm the child. The religious convictions inculcated through early religious education are seen as adult-centered, as incomprehensible for children, and as disturbing or frightening to them. Especially, the references to sin and eternal judgment, to divine punishment, and to being lost for good are prime examples of what, in this view, should never even be mentioned to children.

The popular literature on experiences with religious education in childhood published during the last thirty or forty years is full of examples for this critique of the blend of paternal authority and piety, and, more recently, the issue of the religious background of child abuse has been added to this.[13] In his book *The Quest for Identity*, published in the late 1950s, psychoanalyst Allen Wheelis reports the following scene: Seven-year-old Larry is given the duty of saying the blessing before meals:

> Sometimes…the end of the blessing would be followed by stinging reprimand. "Sit yourself up straight at that table, sir!" After a moment of bewilderment and fright Larry would realize that he had been slouching in his chair, and would stiffen straightly and wait in silence. "Now you say that blessing again, sir!" He would thus be forced to repeat, and then would falteringly begin to eat, wondering if his father were still watching but afraid to look and find out.[14]

In this scene, religious education is closely associated with obedience, with being forced to follow a stern father's commands, and with being deeply frightened. It is easy to imagine how blessings or prayer in general will have become frightful experiences for this young boy, and also how his image of God will have turned out to be anything but friendly or forgiving.

Although of different cultural backgrounds, numerous similar reports are also available from other countries. For example, in Germany, Tilmann Moser coined the much quoted phrase of "God poisoning"—of God having been used as a poison in his parents' ways of nurturing him.[15] Parental love was thus always conditioned by the child's willingness to obey God and to fulfill the diffuse mixture of parental and divine expectations: *Your parents love you if you love God; God loves you if you love your parents; God loves you when you do well; God won't love you if you do not succeed, and so forth.*

A similarly detrimental experience is reported by Monika Schaefer, who, as a little girl, always had to pray with her mother.[16] If she asked God to forgive her for her wrongdoings, she could be sure that her mother would ask her what exactly she had done wrong. And in case little Monika did not ask for God's forgiveness, the mother would helpfully remind her of what she might have forgotten in her prayers. For her, there was no way out of this oppressive ritual that kept repeating itself every night in the name of God's love.

As we will see in the next section, such experiences still play an important role in the present—not because this style of raising children would still be widely practiced but because today's parents are eager to avoid everything that could, even remotely, resemble the type of religious upbringing that most of them remember with terrible feelings from their own childhood days. In other words, the negative experiences with an oppressive religious education are a powerful motive for parents to make sure that the patterns of their childhood days will not repeat themselves for their own children.

Another critical view of the modern understanding of the life cycle is focused on the role of the mother as the so-called primary caregiver of the child. The mother in early childhood, so the critical argument runs, is described with idealized images that are distorted and that make it difficult for any mother to be her true self.[17] According to the idealized image, the mother is the always-loving provider of food, comfort, and safety. And when the mother does not live up to this ideal (which, in reality, will be the case more often than not), the danger of early religious trauma is imminent. A "not good enough" mother becomes responsible for the child's future alienation from faith. Feelings of guilt are the consequence for the mother.

While the idealized view of the mother may not be found with academic psychologists like Erikson, it has nevertheless permeated the popular literature and shaped the consciousness of many people. So the modern understanding of childhood religion is actually not without internal tension. On the one hand, it praises the firm sense of belonging to the faith of one's parents while, on the other hand, it criticizes all religious education in childhood because it can overpower the child. In addition, the parents, especially the mother, are overburdened with unrealistic expectations of acting as an early model for what later may become the explicit image of God.

Most likely, such tensions or ambivalences refer back directly and indirectly to modernity's general ambivalence toward religion. While religion is appreciated as an indispensable basis for moral education, it is also seen as prerational and as unenlightened—as something only for children and maybe for the elderly but not in any case, as will be pointed out in chapter 5 of this book, for the autonomous adult, which modern culture has painted as its grand ideal. Yet while the modern view of childhood can be criticized as ambivalent, it still has permeated much of our thinking about childhood and religion. It still is the basis for many people's expectations when they worry about the changes connected to postmodernity, which we will now consider.

Growing Up in a Plural Postmodern Context

The traditional view of childhood religion as a solid basis for an entire lifetime obviously does not hold true any more. The feeling of being led onto the one right path to truth during childhood by one's parents has become a rare exception for today's children. Instead, the experience of religious plurality has entered the picture, and this experience seems to begin very early. And in addition to this, even in childhood religion is treated as a private affair that is left to the individual. Many parents feel that their child should be given a free choice of what religious convictions he or she wants to adopt and what religious practisces are to his or her liking.[18] And in many cases, conversations within the family seem to stay away from religious topics. Religion obviously is viewed as an intimate matter that cannot be openly addressed, not even within the family.

As educational institutions like nursery schools and kindergartens have become more and more widespread and are attended by the majority of children, the exposure of young children to members of other cultures and of different religious communities has automatically also become a common experience. Such educational institutions often bring together children from all kinds of different backgrounds. And even if the curriculum of these institutions does not openly address religion, children will most likely learn about religious differences from the conversations with their peers.

So from early on children are—or, at least, they may be—aware that everything they learn from their parents can also be seen in very different ways. Some children go to church and some do not, some families pray and others do not, some children learn about Jesus and others do not, some learn about Muhammad, still others about Shiva and Vishnu, while some do not even know the word *God.* It is indeed hard to imagine that there can still be a firm grounding in a single faith tradition of the family in the sense in which this could have been expected at other times. Rather, from early on, there is the experience of religious diversity, of different options and opinions.

Yet do parents even wish for such a firm grounding, as used to be expected? So far, my description of the contemporary situation was implicitly based on the perspective of parents and families that are actively engaged in nurturing their children religiously or that at least would like to see their children being raised in a particular faith. In many cases, however, this is not the case anymore today, at least not in the traditional sense. Among today's parents, many are not affiliated with any religious community, and among those who are, there also seem to be a fair number of people who are very hesitant to introduce their children to any particular religious tradition.[19] Often, there is a fear of indoctrinating the child or of overpowering the child—the fear that, as pointed out above, must be understood in light of not only modern philosophies of education, which tend to emphasize the autonomy of the child, but also of the parents' generation's experiences with religious education in their own childhood.[20] Many of today's parents associate religious education and nurture with authoritarian behavior, with inculcating fixed beliefs, and with planting fears of punishment into the children's hearts. Obviously, today's parents want to avoid repeating the kind of religious education that they themselves once received. The generation that has struggled to free itself from what was widely experienced as paternal or societal authoritarianism is more than eager to avoid whatever might resemble religious authority. In his book *Life after God,* Douglas Coupland, one of the much-discussed authors of the 1990s and on Generation X, speaks of the "first generation raised without religion":

> I began to wonder what exactly I had believed in up until now…This is not an easy thing to do. Precisely articulating one's beliefs is difficult. My own task had been made more difficult because I had been raised without religion by parents who had broken with their own past…—who had raised their children clean of any ideology.[21]

This quotation also shows that we have to become aware of the specific historical location of religious education today. It is the often rebellious adolescents and young adults of the 1960s who have now reached their forties, fifties, or even early sixties. To some extent, it is even the generation of their sons and daughters who make up today's parents of young children. Unless these sons and daughters of the first antiauthoritarian parent generation nevertheless experienced an authoritarian education, which, given the revolt against all demands of obedience in the 1960s and early 1970s, is not very likely, their parents must have been successful in handing on their strong dislike for anything that might look like indoctrination.

Beyond those who want to nurture their children religiously and also beyond those who do not, there is a third group of parents that also seems to be rapidly growing.[22] More and more, we are not only dealing with denominational diversity within families—we are also dealing with religious differences in the sense that, for example, one parent is Muslim, the other Christian, or one parent is Jewish, the other Christian, and so forth. It has been claimed, for example, in a controversial statement by the well-known Harvard theologian Harvey Cox, that, at least with Judaism and Christianity, some kind of dual religious education should be possible.[23] As a matter of fact, however, we know very little about the educational style that is operative in such families. In any case, religious education in a bireligious family does not always seem easy. Martha Fay reports the case of a divorced couple in Colorado:

> The husband...was...Jewish, the wife a Catholic who had converted to Judaism at the time of their marriage. After several years and the birth of two daughters, the parents were divorced. The wife was awarded custody of the girls, who by that time had begun attending Hebrew school, and presumably thought of themselves as Jewish. Soon after the divorce, however, the mother reconsidered her earlier conversion, returned to Catholicism, and eventually married a Catholic. While continuing to take her daughters to Hebrew school on Saturday, she also began taking them to mass on Sunday, claiming the girls were entitled to be exposed to both faiths. The father didn't see it that way and sued for the exclusive right to determine his children's religious training. As his lawyer put it in a newspaper interview, "Either Jesus is the Messiah or he is not."[24]

This report may sound extreme, and it certainly offers no sufficient basis for judging the situation of bireligious or multireligious families. Yet, the report makes one wonder how different religious convictions that often are deeply rooted in one's personality or biography can actually go together with intimately sharing one's life with another person and a whole family. And even if academic theologians have developed an entire body of literature on a more dialogical attitude toward other religions,[25] this attitude is rarely related to matters of everyday life or to religious nurture and education within a family.

One of my doctoral students, Regine Froese, is doing research on religious education in Christian-Muslim families.[26] Her approach is empirical, including interview conversations with children as well as with adults. As she points out on the basis of her preliminary results, a highly internalized and privatized religion may well be the consequence of growing up with a dual religious family background. According to her observations, parents often fear that clearly addressing potentially divisive religious issues like how to celebrate Christmas, Easter, Hanukkah, or Ramadan might lead to family conflicts that parents feel cannot be resolved. So if the alternative is as clear as the lawyer quoted above has it—either Jesus is the Messiah or he is not—the families, for the sake of peace, may prefer to avoid the issue altogether rather than getting themselves into a conflict over matters that are beyond them anyway. Obviously, to stay together as a married couple and to openly disagree on fundamental issues of faith is experienced as contradictory. It seems safer to base life together on religiously neutral grounds and make all religious decisions a private question for the individual members of the family, be they the adults or the children.

The experience of growing up in a context of cultural and religious diversity is certainly challenging enough—with religious plurality as part of everyday life even in childhood and possibly even in one's own family, and with a parent generation (and sometimes also a grandparent generation) that is reluctant to commit their children to a particular faith. Yet the postmodern situation clearly holds more challenges than we have mentioned so far. Probably one of the deepest challenges to the traditional image of childhood as a safe beginning of the life cycle is the increasing number of so-called incomplete or postfamilial families.[27] High divorce rates—over 50 percent in the United States—and second or third marriages are only the most visible signs of how rare the experience of growing up in a stable and continuous family context has become. The so-called primary caregivers of a child, which were so important for the traditional modern view of religious nurture in the family, may thus be changed once, or even several times during the first decade of life.

Unfortunately, there are no psychological accounts or empirical data that would indicate what such so-called postfamilial situations mean for the religious development of the child. The classical models from psychoanalysis, for example, are premised on the child's continuous relationships with mother and father. So it will be a very important task for future research to find out if and how the maternal and paternal roots of the child's image of God are actually affected by the postmodern changes of the family. Or, to put it in a more general way, if the experience of divorce is becoming more and more widespread, we also need to look into the psychological consequences for religious education and nurture—a question that has not received the attention it deserves.

It is obvious that much more could be said about contemporary childhood experiences. For example, the influence of the media on religious nurture has also not really been investigated. But enough has been said to make clear beyond any doubt that the traditional modern expectations regarding religion in childhood are no longer warranted. It is a pressing issue to think anew about the tasks of church and theology vis-à-vis such challenges.

Children's Right to Religion: Perspectives between Belonging and Openness

How are we to judge the changes taking place with the postmodern life cycle? How are we to respond to the changing religious situation of childhood? Much of the literature is focused on the issue of diversity.[28] Two conflicting views or ideals dominate the picture. On the one hand, there is a very positive attitude toward religious plurality in childhood because it is seen as the presupposition for tolerance and for a new openness toward other religions. On the other hand, there is apprehension and fear that children may no longer be able to acquire a firm sense of belonging to a religious community and to a clearly identified tradition of faith. Ideals of multicultural and multireligious richness stand against the danger of religious homelessness. Which understanding may we trust? And what are the consequences we should pursue?

In my understanding, the standard analysis of the contemporary situation just presented does not go far enough. Religious homelessness is not only a result of multicultural influences. Today it is also, and probably most of all, a consequence of an insufficient or absent religious nurture and education. By themselves, many families feel unable (or are unwilling) to take responsibility for this kind of nurture and education. This is why the tension between religious belonging and openness actually is not the first question to be addressed. Before this question, there is an even deeper issue to be taken up—the possibility that many children in postmodernity may not receive any truly religious education at all.

To be sure, all children have religious questions or at least questions that are potentially religious. Yet the fear of indoctrinating children, together with an often materialistic outlook, may silence even the biggest questions that children ask. Douglas Coupland, whose book *Life after God* I already quoted, again relates a telling conversation with a child:

> You asked questions about the animals, some real toughies, and these questions came as a welcome diversion...Just after you saw the eagle you asked me, seemingly out of the blue, "*Where do people come from?*" I wasn't sure if you meant the birds and bees or if you meant the ark or what have you. Either direction was a tad too much for me to handle just then...You repeated your question again and so I gave you a makeshift answer of the sort parents aren't supposed to give. I told you people came "from back east."[29]

Against the backdrop of such answers—or, more exactly, of avoiding an answer altogether—I see a clear need to address children's right to religion. As I have tried to show elsewhere, children have a right to religion because they need religious education if they are to grow up in a healthy way.[30] And in my understanding, this view may be defended theologically as well as psychologically.

The theological reasons are quite obvious. Beginning with the Bible, the call to share the faith with the children has always been present in the Jewish as well as in the Christian tradition. Deuteronomy 6:20–21 is often seen as the classic expression:

> When your children ask you..."What is the meaning of the decrees and the statutes and the ordinances that the LORD our God has commanded you?" then you shall say to your children, "We were Pharaoh's slaves in Egypt, but the LORD brought us out of Egypt with a mighty hand."

And in Mark 10:14b, we hear Jesus say:

> "Let the little children come to me; do not stop them; for it is to such as these that the kingdom of God belongs."

Even if children's rights have not always been respected, from today's point of view it cannot be doubted theologically that children have a right to religion.[31] But the child's right to religion may also be stated on psychological grounds. As we have seen above from the psychoanalytic account, the child's early experiences always include a religious dimension. The process of being recognized by mother or father, as in a mirror that affirms—or denies—the child's personal existence, is of ultimate meaning and may therefore be called religious. If this holds true, we may further conclude that there also is a need for giving the child a language that is capable of expressing such experiences or of at least addressing them and communicating with others. Otherwise, a whole dimension of human existence will be excluded from communication. And communication here is also the presupposition for healing what has gone wrong during childhood and for supporting children in finding meaning for their lives. Only if early experiences of denial can be addressed, will it be possible to correct them and to give a person the affirmation needed for becoming a healthy self.

It should be noted that, with this understanding, we are also trying to overcome the modern ambivalence between the idealization of childhood religion on the one hand and the critique of religious nurture as indoctrination on the other. In line with a postmodern view of the child, we are viewing the child as an active subject—a person who is processing a wide variety of experiences within his or her natural, interpersonal, and symbolic environment. If we take this view seriously, children need access to an environment that offers religious symbols and narratives as forms of religious communication. It is in this sense that children have a right to religion and to religious nurture.

Who is to safeguard this right to religion? Traditionally, the family could have been expected to do this. Given that children continue to need families, the potential contribution of the family to religious nurture is an additional reason for church and theology to support parents in this respect. At the same time, it becomes increasingly important that church and theology come to realize their special responsibility for children. As mentioned above, there are sound theological reasons for this special responsibility. The insecure status of religious nurture and education makes it a pressing issue to act upon this responsibility by becoming much more intentional about children in the congregation. Sunday school programs, if taken seriously, are a good beginning. But it may well turn out that there is a need for new and additional programs and structures for children if the challenges of the contemporary situation are to be seriously tackled. Most of all, we must learn to see the congregation not only as adults and for adults, but through the eyes of children and with their needs in mind.

Taking the child's perspective can also shed new light on the postmodern tension between belonging and openness. Logically, the opposite poles of the tension between religious belonging and openness may be mutually exclusive. If we take the point of view of the child, they are not. If it is a right of children that their big questions are listened to and that adults offer them whatever they believe to be the most honest and most trustworthy answers to such questions, then religious education will always work toward a sense of belonging and of grounding a young person in a certain religious tradition. This is not to deny the influence of religious individualization on adults' beliefs and outlooks mentioned earlier. Yet if we want to be responsible educators, we will have to check our individual and personal answers against the insights of those who, for hundreds and thousands of years, have studied the religious sources and who have thought and argued over their understanding. So in this sense, religious belonging as an aim of Christian education has not lost its importance because of postmodernity.

But this is only one side of the coin. There can be no reasonable grounds for advocating a close-minded approach in the sense of a new denominationalism or confessionalism. Even if there are good reasons for the need for grounding and belonging, we cannot overlook that children are constantly exposed to the experience of religious plurality. The only way to exclude this experience would be to lock up the children on an island, thus reenacting the ancient dream of creating a purely educational province sheltered from society. Once we drop this dream because it may not be put into practice and also because it is not really desirable to isolate our children from the world, we have to ask how the actual and inevitable experience of religious plurality may become most fruitful for children.

With this understanding, we are in position to leave behind the paralyzing alternatives that modernity forces upon us. In postmodernity, there is no choice to be made between religious belonging and openness as it is mistakenly suggested by the literature. And there is also no choice between an idealized childhood religion and religious indoctrination. Rather, we have to accept the child as an active center of experience and as a person who, from early on, is faced with experiences shaped by the environment. The task of Christian education, then, is to be with the child and to support the child in this process of dealing with his or her experiences. In postmodernity, the aim of education can neither be a return to an unquestioned state of natural belonging nor can it be only openness, which actually is quite impossible without a center of belonging. Rather, it is the balance between religious belonging and openness for which we have to strive by stressing, at the same time, a firm sense of being grounded in the Christian faith, as well as the capacity to accept and to affirm the faith of others as different from one's own.

This view of childhood religious education as a dynamic process may also help us to get beyond the ideological image of the modern family. While it remains true and important that children need reliable families as a place where they can grow up, this need must also be reconciled with the inevitable realities of family life. There is no use in casting the behavior of mothers or fathers in idealistic terms by seeing them as all-loving and ever caring persons. Quite the opposite, such ideal images only indicate the dangerous tendency to deify parents by giving them divine attributes. Rather than supporting this ideological process, theology and Christian education need to base their understanding of religious education on a critical and realistic view of what experiences the child will have during his or her first years of life.

These considerations are not meant to deny the enormous problems that we have to face with the postmodern family and, more specifically, with the disintegration of the family through divorce and similar developments. Rather, I want to point out that the modern family should not be seen naïvely and that it should also not be seen as the indispensable presupposition for Christian nurture. Modern childhood was certainly not the realization of an ideal childhood. Consequently, we must come to see that religious education in postmodern childhood does not only mean loss and imbalance.

In sum, then, I perceive three challenges for church and theology today:

- Much more must be done for children in church and congregation. New and additional programs are needed that are geared to religious nurture and education. And this presupposes that church and theology come to realize their special responsibility for children.
- Church and theology should become advocates for children's right to religion. This right is not a legal question in the first place. It is about nurture and education, and it is about how children are viewed in church and society, in the praxis of education as well as in academic discourse. Children need our support so that their religious questions and needs are no longer overlooked and bypassed by a society that is focused on questions of rationality and materialistic needs.
- Theology and the church must work toward a new balance between belonging and openness. This balance is demanding. It requires new intellectual capacities for dealing with issues like conflicting religious truth claims, but it also requires social and relational skills in welcoming others who are different from one's own group. There is no healthy way back to the naïve and unquestioned sense of belonging that was possibly found in the past. But openness alone is also not possible, because it would mean giving up one's own identity.

CHAPTER 3

In Search of a Faith of One's Own
The Identity of Plural Selves in Adolescence

As we move along the life cycle beyond childhood, which was the topic of chapter 2, we encounter adolescence—the topic of the present chapter. With adolescence, we also encounter the stage of the life cycle that, in the time of postmodernity, seems to be the most worrisome time for many people in church and society. Most of all during adolescence, the experience of pluriformity and dissolution seems to affect the process of growing up by exposing young people to the impact of plurality, competing worldviews, or, maybe more accurately, the opaqueness of uncertainty vis-à-vis all too many options.

Growing Up Postmodern: Imitating Christ in the Age of "Whatever" was the telling theme of the 1998 Princeton Lectures on Youth, Church, and Culture.[1] Headlines like "Youth without God" or "The Patchwork Religion of Adolescence" are similar expressions to be found in Germany or other European countries.[2] Obviously, there is a widespread concern about what is really happening in adolescence today. Moreover, it is an open question if and how church and theology may become able to address the changing situation of postmodern youth. The well-known question, "Will our children have faith?" really applies to the adolescents much more than to children who, even today, are much more likely to go along with what they receive from their parents.[3]

Such concerns about youth and about the religious outlooks and affiliations of adolescents are often based on practical experiences in youth ministry and Christian education. Sometimes they are based on survey data resulting from interview studies with youth or the general population.[4] So in a sense, such views are just obvious, at least to the immediate observer, and the only question is about possible consequences for Christian education, which has to find new ways of communicating and staying in touch with adolescents. I certainly share this practical concern. Yet in the context of our present analysis, additional aspects come to the fore that bring us back to the questions of modernity and postmodernity. As will become clear throughout this chapter, dealing with these questions is a presupposition for successful Christian education and youth ministry.

In my view, there are specific reasons why successful practical approaches can only come from a deeper analysis of the situation in this case. Many observations and concerns about contemporary youth are implicitly or explicitly based on certain expectations, and these expectations often seem to be modeled on the modern life cycle. In this case, the modern model—which now, with the arrival of postmodernity, has become the traditional one—exerts a defining influence on how today's adults in church and society encounter today's adolescents. If this is true, the encounter between the generations cannot be very successful. Judging postmodern youth by the standards of modernity does not allow for the specific needs and longings that are connected to today's situation. This is why we have to become clear about the changes to be observed with youth.

In light of this, it makes sense to again follow the three-step procedure that I described in the preceding chapters. I will first take stock by looking at the modern life cycle and the religious expectations connected to youth in the modern view. After this, I will ask about the changes that may be observed when modern adolescence is compared with today's experiences, especially with respect to religion in adolescence. In a final step, I will take up the question of how theology and the church may respond to the challenges that arise from the changing face of adolescence.

Traditional Modern Expectations: Faith and Identity in Adolescence

It is quite common in the literature for social scientists and educators to speak of "modern adolescence." Sometimes, they also speak of "modern childhood" or of "modern adulthood," but the references to "modern adolescence" are much more frequent and widespread. Obviously, there is a special connection between adolescence and modernity, and this connection is of special interest if we want to know about the transformations leading to postmodern adolescence.

When researchers speak of "modern adolescence," the reference to modernity often has a dual meaning. The first meaning is easy to understand: In modernity, adolescence took on a particular character that was different from earlier forms of passing through this age. In this case, we just have to think of modern culture in general and of how it influences everyday life, through the media; cars and other twentieth-century means of transportation; the availability of goods; the impact of science and technology; and so forth. Through all of this, adolescence has changed, just as other segments of the life cycle. In this sense, there is no difference between modern adolescence and, say, modern adulthood. Yet there is a second meaning of the reference to "modern adolescence": Historians speak of the historical emergence or even of the discovery of adolescence in modernity.[5] According to this view, there was no adolescence before modernity, at least not as a distinct phase of life. After childhood, which was also much less well-defined in earlier times, came adulthood—or, rather, came the kind of integrated life that everyone shared, quite independent of one's age.

To be sure, in most cultures, even in so-called primitive ones, there are puberty rites that typically mark and dramatize the passage into adulthood. The ushering function of such rites has been studied extensively in anthropology and, at least in some sense, these studies of transitional rituals have remained influential as a background for contemporary theories of adolescent development.[6] In this sense, there is a certain continuity concerning the different shapes of adolescence across human history. It is overdone to speak of adolescence as a modern invention. But it is also obvious that the continuity does not speak against the observation of discontinuities and changes, which may, in fact, by far outweigh the continuity. In so-called primitive cultures, transitional rites did not create a phase of life. Often, they were to be completed within a few days' time, and, after that, the status of adulthood was achieved.[7] Some of the rites described in the literature included a few days in a different environment and away from one's family; often there were special foods involved or special tasks that had to be completed by the young participants. In today's language, such rites and the experience that they create are closer to an event than to a stage of life. Today, wedding ceremonies can possibly be seen as a similar case. Such ceremonies also have an ushering function in that they mark the passage into married life. And although some kind of ceremony is constitutive for a marriage to come into existence, the wedding is an event and not a phase of life. In a similar manner, adolescent rites of passages can be seen as events ushering in adulthood.

One of the most important factors responsible for the historically late emergence of adolescence as a distinct stage within the life cycle is the scarcity of educational institutions in earlier history and cultures. Only with the introduction of mandatory schooling beyond the age of ten was there a social and institutional basis for adolescence to become a general experience in today's sense, and this kind of schooling is largely a twentieth-century innovation. Only a small part of the younger generation attended school on a regular basis before that.

Of course, the *idea* of modern adolescence antedates its becoming a general experience that did not happen before the twentieth century.[8] The understanding of adolescence as a quick passage from childhood to adulthood begins to change with the onset of modernity in the eighteenth century. From the perspective of the history of ideas, the clearest example can be found with the French philosopher Jean-Jacques Rousseau, who is also one of the classical thinkers of modern education. In his *Émile,* published in 1762, Rousseau speaks of adolescence as a "second birth."[9] He sees it as the birth into real life, because adolescence brings about the intellectual and emotional capacities needed for a life that, in his view, goes beyond mere existence. With the idea of a "second birth," adolescence is given an unprecedented meaning. Rousseau made adolescence the true center of the modern life cycle.

Ideas such as Rousseau's also became the basis for a new understanding of education. For the most part, modern education is premised on the idea of the autonomous self that is to be achieved in adolescence. And with more and more children and youth attending school for longer and longer periods of time, a prolonged phase of transition between childhood and adulthood was established as a general pattern, at least in Western countries. In this sense, adolescence is indeed a modern innovation—a late addition to the human life cycle. To put it figuratively: Adolescence is a child of the twentieth century. It is the twin sister of compulsory schooling and the twin brother of the concomitant abolition of child labor, setting children free for the school.

So does this mean that adolescence has nothing to do with puberty in the sense of physiology or psychology? Is adolescence only the result of social circumstances? This kind of reductionist view would certainly be wrong. But it makes sense to understand adolescence contextually by being aware of the social, historical, and institutional factors that define or even create the space in which the physiological and psychological processes can take place and in which they take on a certain shape. It is no coincidence that academic theories of adolescence did not really exist before the twentieth century. G. Stanley Hall's *Adolescence, its Psychology and its Relations to Physiology, Anthropology, Sociology, Sex, Crime, Religion, and Education* was published in 1905.[10] And in spite of its sometimes questionable content, this book is considered an important starting point for the modern psychology of adolescence. In any case, it is an early milestone on the way to this kind of academic endeavor that since then has become so widespread and commonplace.

Hall's work at the beginning of the century was innovative but, considering its reception, it did not furnish a solid basis for the new psychological task of understanding adolescent development. If we are looking for a psychological understanding of modern adolescence that became most widely accepted, we may again turn to Erik Erikson, whose model of the life cycle can once more serve as a backdrop for my analysis. With his books, especially *Youth and Crisis* and *Young Man Luther,* Erikson became a real prophet of modern adolescence.[11] His books not only informed psychologists and sociologists, parents, teachers, and educators, but they also reached an adolescent audience that sometimes was eager to use such concepts as *identity* and *identity crisis* for their own self-understanding. Literary figures such as James Joyce's Stephen Daedalus or Hermann Hesse's Demian, both described in novels that became very popular in the 1960s and 1970s, reflect and support this kind of adolescent self-understanding on a symbolic level.[12]

The core of Erikson's model of adolescent development is the assumption that the young person, upon entering the stage of adolescence, critically tests and, in part, rejects all identifications that he or she acquired during childhood. And according to Erikson, this process is by no means only negative, rejective, or even destructive (although it may look and feel that way at certain times). Rather, it is the precondition for what Erikson envisions as the true result or aim of adolescent development: a new and more independent identity. This kind of identity can only be achieved, Erikson maintains, after the adolescent has become free from the identifications taken over in childhood without, at that time, having been able to test and to examine them in an independent manner. Thus, the new identity to be acquired in adolescene is based upon earlier experiences, but it is more than the sum of all of them. Erikson views it as a new synthesis of elements, which are appropriated under the condition that the autonomous self can accept—or reject—them as appropriate or inappropriate.

According to this view, adolescent identity formation means at least partial independence from one's past. At the same time, the identity to be achieved in adolescence is seen as the basis for one's future. All developments that come after adolescence are in some way based on the transformation of childhood experiences, which is the main developmental task for the second decade of life. In this respect, Erikson's view is similar to that of Rousseau: With both of them, adolescence has become the fulcrum of the life cycle.[13]

Yet, modern adolescence was not only a question of philosophy, psychology, or of the inner feelings and individual experiences of young people. Sociologists such as Talcott Parsons joined the psychological debate on adolescence by pointing out that it is modern society itself that makes adolescence necessary.[14] From a sociological and functionalist point of view, modern science and technology require years of education and training before a young person can join the adult work force. And with this requirement, adolescence comes into being as a societal requirement, that is, in order to fulfill the task of preparing people for adult work. It is important to keep this social background of the emergence of adolescence as a stage of life in mind. The changes connected to our contemporary situation do not only affect psychological aspects, but they are also related, for example, to the career expectations of the younger generation and to the societal institutions that exert their influence by shaping and backing these expectations.

The psychological and sociological presuppositions of modern adolescence that I have presented so far are fairly well known, and the views reported above are commonly accepted among researchers on youth. However, the religious background of the emergence of modern adolescence has not received much attention at all. It is, in fact, a rather new development that historical studies on youth have become aware of this background and have come to include references to the history of Christianity with their accounts of the history of youth.[15] Even readers who are theologically informed may consider it surprising that there should be a historical link between the emergence of adolescence and the church. In what sense, then, is there a link? The pertinent studies point to a special influence of Protestantism and of the Protestant use of the rite of confirmation.[16] It is, indeed, easy to see that confirmation did not become a general practice in many Protestant churches until early modernity. In Europe, confirmation was introduced in most Protestant churches sometime during the eighteenth century, and this religious rite celebrated in the second decade of life, often around the age of fourteen or fifteen, influenced the understanding of adolescence. In many cases, especially with German pietism as well as with the Enlightenment, confirmation was associated with the expectation of a personal profession of faith that sometimes took on the shape of a formal religious oath. Through this, confirmation became a time of religious passage leading into adult faith—the faith of an autonomous individual who takes over responsibility for this faith himself (and, at that time, only sometimes herself). This view of confirmation had important implications for how young people were seen and treated within the family and within society. For example, certain kinds of work were reserved for the time after confirmation, which implies that the general introduction of confirmation marked off a period of life without full participation in working life. In sum, the introduction of confirmation into Protestantism created a new awareness of adolescence: It tended to associate this time of life with positive expectations, and it helped in demarcating a place for it in the human life cycle.

Confirmation is, of course, only one example of how Christianity has been related to the historical emergence of adolescence. Studies on twentieth-century adolescence have pointed to the special role that Christian youth work has played in defining modern adolescence.[17] In this case, expectations of religious and moral development were operative in defining adolescence as a time for education, which again shows that theology and the church have had an inherent interest in the existence and shape of this time of life. As a time for education and personal development, adolescence can afford the individual person many more possibilities for becoming a responsible Christian as well as a responsible member of the community than commonly were available before the new definition of this age came into the picture.

Erikson's model of identity formation has received much attention from theology. His ideas have been taken up by theological anthropologists and also by various theorists of pastoral counseling as well as of Christian education.[18] Especially in the practical fields, Erikson plays the role of something like a classic. What makes his model so interesting for theologians is not primarily the wide attention that it has received from various academic and popular audiences. Rather, it is Erikson's claim that successful identity formation is always premised on a worldview that must be available to the adolescent.[19] This worldview is needed to give adolescents a sense of their meaningful position in society and in history.[20] With this, Erikson does not, of course, suggest that all adolescents should come to see themselves as preeminent historical figures, which, psychologically speaking, would be a narcissistic delusion. But what adolescents need, according to Erikson, is a chance to make sense of their lives and to find some kind of meaningful purpose. This psychological requirement gives faith or religion a clear place in the human life cycle—an idea that is intrinsically attractive for theologians because it connects their views and perspectives to human life. Adolescent development is in need of being supported by meaningful interpretations of society and history, and religion seems to fit perfectly this developmental need. Or, to quote Erikson himself, in adolescence

> an ideological formula, intelligible both in terms of individual development and of significant tradition, must do for the young person what the mother did for the infant: provide nutriment for the soul as well as for the stomach, and screen the environment so that vigorous growth may meet what it can manage.[21]

At first sight, this quotation sounds as though Erikson would consider any "ideological" understanding to be equally helpful in adolescence, provided it "screens the environment" by interpreting or ordering it for the adolescent. But it should not be overlooked that Erikson does, in fact, speak of a "significant tradition" on which such understandings should be based. And Erikson can be quite outspoken in recommending a crucial role for what he calls humanism in adolescence.[22] In the 1960s, when he developed his theory, he expected this humanism to have an important role to play for the future of culture and society, which needed to be protected against totalitarianism as well as against the overwhelming reductionist influence of science and technology.[23] Following this understanding, it is possible, at least from my point of view, to see the Christian faith with its strong humanizing potential as a worldview on which adolescents can base their identities. If this is true, the Christian faith can be understood as supporting the future of humankind against the reduction to an exclusively technological vision.

Such critical evaluations of technology and its possible abuse remind us of the fact that Erikson was by no means a naïve modern thinker. In some ways, his critical visions foreshadow some of what later came to be called postmodernism or a second (self-critical) modernity. Given today's debates, for example, on biotechnologies and on their potential for perfecting the human being, it seems obvious to me that Erikson's tenets about the humanizing influence that a corresponding worldview should exert on technology are still important to church and theology. Yet just as with other concepts developed under the auspices of modernity, his notion of identity also contains ambivalence that should not be overlooked. I will take up this ambivalence in the next section, which addresses the postmodern challenge of a plural self.

The Postmodern Challenge of a Plural Self

In recent times, the modern—or traditional—understanding of identity and religion in adolescence has been challenged on two levels. On the one hand, it has been pointed out that the contemporary social and religious situation differs drastically from the time and situation in which the modern psychological idea of identity was set forth.[24] We are now living in a new century or even in a new millennium, and the lifestyles of the 1960s have little in common with the lifestyles after the year 2000. So in this view, the modern idea of identity is outdated because of far-reaching historical changes that make it difficult or even impossible to hold on to this idea. On the other hand, it has been claimed that the modern notion of identity was ideological from the beginning. It never held true for many, if not most, people's experiences. Here, the modern understanding of identity is seen as individualistic and also as a description of exclusively male adolescent development.[25]

Let us begin by looking at the social and religious situation with its implications for the formation of identity. Here, a first challenge arises from the observation that adolescence itself has again changed its character during the last few decades.[26] The changes to which I am referring are not only superficial changes concerning, for example, the preference for certain types of clothing, certain foods, or certain kinds of popular culture. The changes that need to be considered in the present context go much deeper. They affect, for example, what may be called the temporal substructures of adolescence. In order to understand the far-reaching consequences of such changes, we must remind ourselves of the crucial importance of a time perspective within the emergence of adolescence. Modernity created adolescence as a period of transition marked off against childhood and against adulthood. No longer a child and not yet an adult: This was the modern understanding. Childhood is the time before adolescence, and adulthood is the time after it. What seems to have happened since then is that the "not yet" has come under question, and this for a variety of simultaneous reasons. First, the perspective of working life has changed. The idea of preparing oneself during adolescence for a particular type of adult work is not always realistic anymore.

Many countries of the world have gone through extended periods with high rates of so-called youth unemployment—a term that really means that for many there is no work after adolescence, an unresolved problem that is widely discussed, for example, in Germany.[27] And even in those countries that, like the United States at this point, do not suffer as much from unemployment, the jobs offered to many young people hardly qualify as lifetime careers, unless one wants to see selling hamburgers and hot dogs as a meaningful perspective for life (a perspective that, in any case, does not require much preparation).[28] Moreover, with most higher level jobs, life-long learning and job flexibility have become mandatory. So no longer is there one period of life that could be marked off as the period of learning. It is much more accurate to say that life as a whole has become a continuous time for learning and training.

The effects that these changes have exerted on adolescence are manifold. For example, adolescence tends to stretch out more and more—with postadolescence as a new stage of the life cycle (see chapter 4), or simply with young people not leaving adolescence behind. In Europe, it has become customary for studies on youth to include thirty-year-olds, and some researchers have even discussed the idea of including thirty- to forty-year-olds as well! At the same time, many things that used to be reserved for adults have now been claimed by adolescents—sexual relationships or a high degree of personal independence, to mention only two examples. All of this creates a different sense of time and a different perspective on the stages of the life cycle ahead of oneself. This is why I said that the temporal substructures of adolescence are no longer what they used to be at the time when psychologists such as Erikson alerted us to the formation of identity in adolescence.

These changes of adolescence and of its position within the life cycle make it less and less likely that anything like a firm sense of identity may develop during the second decade of life as Erikson supposed. Rather, identity formation turns out to be a flexible and, most likely, a lifelong process. As the experience of transitional periods in life has multiplied—with changes of profession, new trainings, second and third marriages, and so forth—the need to rework and to reestablish one's identity has also become an enduring task never to be quite completed.

The changing temporal aspects of identity can create very difficult problems for the people who go through these changes. Yet there is an even more far-reaching and pervasive challenge to the modern understanding of identity, which has to do with plurality as one of the main characteristics of our contemporary situation. There has always been agreement that identity is related to social roles and to the recognition of the self by others. But what does it mean if the various roles that people play in their everyday lives multiply and are constantly changing, and if there is no center or overarching system to integrate them? This is exactly what social analysts tell us about the contemporary situation. In adolescence (and also in adulthood), the plurality of situational expectations has clearly multiplied: families, schools, different peer groups, consumer situations, the influence of the media, contacts via the Internet–all of these settings with their relational patterns include more or less defined identities that typically are not related to each other, at least not in a consistent manner. It is easy to see why social scientists have argued that the term "identity" no longer is adequate to capture this experience.[29] Terms like "plural self" or "plural identities" are then suggested in order to include the pluriform experience of the self in adolescence and beyond. Concepts like the plural self are meant to capture the experience of not having just one answer to the question "Who am I?" but several different answers and self-definitions. And the various self-definitions are also not held together or integrated by an overarching synthesis anymore. If there is coherence to the different experiences of the self, it is at best a coherence accompanied by permanent discontinuity.

The cultural and historical challenges to the modern idea of identity that we have considered so far go along with further challenges, which concern the ideological character of modern identity. Here, one of the initial criticisms was set forth by feminist psychology, which suggests that the idea of identity described by Erikson and others was one-sided and distorted from the beginning.[30] In the understanding of psychologists such as Carol Gilligan, Erikson's account of adolescent development stresses only the image of the autonomous independent self, which has to struggle for its freedom against all demands of keeping this self under control.[31] If the struggle for independence comes to be so dominant, Gilligan continues, this kind of self or identity can only be achieved at the expense of the relational self and at the expense of mature dependence. According to this critical view, the assumption that the achievement of a firm identity is the basis for mature intimacy leaves out, and deeply underestimates, the need for interpersonal relationships and for connectedness, which are indispensable for healthy development. Moreover, if identity is always relational, it will never be as unitary and as stable as the traditional account seemed to suggest. Rather, identity always changes with different relationships. So one should speak of a relational self rather than of identity. This feminist critique is raised against Erikson's model independent of its application to men or women. The relational self is considered the more adequate account for both genders. At the same time, so the critical assessment continues, the ideal vision of the autonomous and independent self becomes most distortive and oppressive when it is applied to women.[32] The experience of women is much more relational from the beginning. So it is especially important for girls and women that psychological accounts of adolescent development have space for a relational understanding and for the formation of identity through being connected to others.

In the discussion on postmodern approaches to the self, the critical evaluation of the unitary character of identity has been generalized and radicalized even further. According to this view, there can be no fixed identities under the conditions of postmodern life. The constant flux of roles and situations generates "plural selves" and "plural identities." The image for this kind of self is a patchwork rather than any type of solid material.[33] It is important to note that, just like the relational self, the plural self is not only seen as a reality of contemporary life. Speaking of a plural self is also expressive of a different way of interpreting and of valuing the self. In other words, the reference to the plural self is meant to liberate the person from oppressive expectations of cultural and personal integration, which are seen as connected to the model of the unitary self and of the stable identity (which now is often called a fixed identity). Just as the breakdown of all master stories is seen as making space for the many individual stories, so the breakdown of the unitary model of identity is expected to open up new possibilities for personal and social liberation in that it makes space for the multiple realities of individual life that had to be suppressed in modernity. At least from this critical perspective, the postmodern experience of a plural self is greeted as the final realization that the description of the modern self is not only outdated, but was never in line with the real needs of most people.

The challenges to traditional identity also affect religion in adolescence. Numerous empirical studies from various countries basically show the same picture: Religion in adolescence has become highly pluralized as well as individualized.[34] Sociologists of religion such as Thomas Luckmann speak of a "patchwork religion" as the most likely counterpart of patchwork identities and plural selves.[35] Many adolescents approach religious traditions selectively, picking out one thing from a tradition without bothering about the internal coherence or dignity of this tradition. The Christian teaching of resurrection, for example, is then easily combined with the idea of an immortal soul being reborn several times and in different incarnations. Or a golden cross is added to one's fashionably black clothes because it looks and feels "good" to wear it in this combination.

Beyond such visible outer signs and symbols of religious pluralization, there are the internal processes that relate to the adolescents' ways of formulating their faith. Often, these processes when expressed by youth in open interviews show a clear reluctance to accept the teachings of theology or the church.[36] Many adolescents express their faith by saying that it is their own faith, which is different from the faith of the church. They say that the church is outdated and only their personal faith is of interest to them. It is important to note that they do not consider the difference between the faith of the church and their own faith to be a problem. Rather, they feel that it is quite fine, most acceptable, and only natural that they claim their own versions of a faith. At least on the surface, there is little to nothing left of a general teaching authority as it used to be attributed to church officials and theologians in the past.[37] The fear of being different and therefore of becoming a religious outcast has given way to the feeling that no one has the right to interfere with something as private or intimate as one's personal faith. Interestingly enough, this is not only true for countries such as the United States, where religious individualism and independence from church authorities have always played a major role. It is also true for European countries, even those that had a state church until well into the twentieth century and did not seem to be characterized by religious dissent.[38]

Behind the general attitude of having a faith that is quite different from the church, there often is a widespread skepticism vis-à-vis all truth claims, especially in the field of religion. In a much-read essay by a twenty-year-old German looking at religion in adolescence, this young author voices the understanding that it is quite impossible to say which faith is right and which is wrong, which one is true and which one is not.[39] There are just too many truth claims, he says, too many truth claims to ever test them out. Accordingly, adolescents have become aware of the multitude of different perspectives, of contradictory interpretations and competing explanations. They have grown up with the excessive availability of information and entertainment, be it through printed materials of all kinds, through television, videos, computers, or the Internet. There always seem to be choices, in religion no less than in other fields of life, more choices than can be thoroughly considered.

Another tendency to be observed with adolescents growing up in this postmodern situation is the separation between personal religion or spirituality on the one hand, and the church as an institution on the other. This has been long observed in countries such as Germany, where the church, because of its past as a state church, is a highly organized body of national extension, but it can also be seen in the United States, where the inclination to speak of one's spiritual interests rather than of one's faith or religion is becoming stronger and stronger. Many adolescents in Europe express their interest in personal religion—they believe in an afterlife and they say that they pray—yet all this seems to happen in private and not in connection with worshiping in a congregation.[40] Adolescents often describe church services as cold, impersonal, boring, and as "only for older people." In addition to the emotional distance from the church, there is also a widespread criticism of the church as an institution. Many adolescents feel that the church does not follow its own teachings and that, consequently, it has lost all credibility for them.

It is especially noteworthy that the belief in God seems to play a special role in this situation. Even adolescents who feel alienated from the church and who do not accept the teachings of the church still express a lasting interest in God.[41] Most often, they see themselves struggling with no longer being able to accept what they see as their childhood faith. And yet, many of them want to hold on to God even with all their doubts. A nineteen-year-old woman put it this way:

> For me, God as a person used to be a given for a long time. At some point, I noticed that you cannot limit it to a person, that he becomes too much humanized through that. Then I feel that I need something which I can imagine or which I can picture but that this is not possible for me anymore. Often I feel, in conversation, with other people, outdoors, on a mountain or so—then I really feel that there is a God. But in some situations it is the opposite. Then it is all gone. Then I cannot imagine the person...somehow everything is empty and nothing works.[42]

This statement should also remind us of the fact that the effects of religious development from childhood into adolescence still play their role. There still is the task of coming to terms with the beliefs of one's childhood, of integrating them with the new and different intellectual capacities and outlooks emerging in adolescence, and of finding a new religious stance for the present and for the future. Yet the classic descriptions of religious development as offered, for example, by James Fowler,[43] clearly have to be broadened in order to include the cultural and contextual influences of contemporary religious life. The models of developmental psychology are not necessarily blind to influences from the environment. In the Piagetian tradition in which Fowler, at least in part, developed his stages of faith, the interaction between the person and the environment actually plays a major role. Yet the influence of different environments–of religiously homogenous environments as opposed to religiously plural surroundings, or of isolated cultures as opposed to globalized ones– has not really been studied.[44] Not until recently, and not within the psychology of religion, have there been more substantial attempts to study the development of "meaning making" against the backdrop of the rapid changes of contemporary culture in the United States.[45] And as mentioned in the introductory chapter, such studies have been a very important motivating factor for me to carry this kind of contextual work further by including the contemporary situation of church and religion.

In concluding this section, I want to mention yet another challenge that has not received the attention in the literature that it really deserves. Late adolescence, or as some like to call it, postadolescence, is the prime time for leaving the church–be it for becoming more distant internally or be it for dropping one's church membership altogether.[46] Recently, I reviewed the literature on religion in late adolescence. I was struck by the fact that religious disaffiliation at that particular time of life seems to be a truly international phenomenon. The description of the most likely person to leave the church is very similar in different countries, and it always makes reference to young people. Looking more closely at what "young" means in this context, one often finds the age from about twenty years on. So the time of late adolescence, which has received the least attention in Christian education literature, has actually become the period in the life cycle that poses the most far-reaching challenges to church and theology. This is why I decided to devote a chapter of its own to this new stage of life (see chapter 4) rather than including it with adolescence as one of its latest extensions. But before considering postadolescence more closely, we must ask about the challenges that the changing shape of adolescence holds for church and theology.

Facing Up to Postmodern Adolescence in Church and Theology

Christian youth workers and counselors, as well as ministers and religion teachers, often deplore the difficulties of working with today's adolescents. To them, most of the changes they perceive with young people seem to contradict or even to violate the expectations of the church. Some observers speak of a growing hedonism among youth; others point to the relativism and skepticism that they encounter with this age group.[47] Are today's adolescents a hopeless case—at least for those who are interested in what these adolescents believe and in what they consider true and trustworthy for their own future life?

For me, the frustration of practitioners is very understandable. Christian youth work has certainly become more difficult and demanding. Yet rather than withdrawing from this difficult age group as an easy way out or just condemning the members of the upcoming generation for their immoral behavior and for their lack of interest in the Christian faith, we should at least consider the possibility of a constructive response to the situation of postmodern adolescence. Obviously, being an adolescent today is quite different from what being an adolescent used to mean twenty, thirty, or forty years ago when today's adults were at that stage of life. Consequently, it is to be expected that the different generations will not be able to cooperate or to come to agreements about what is interesting and important in life as long as their different experiences are not taken into consideration. In a situation of rapid change, any constructive response presupposes the careful discernment of new ways of addressing the contemporary forms of life and of religion in adolescence. In my understanding, this includes at least four different tasks for theology and the church.

(1) A first task refers to the *changing shape of adolescence* as a period of life. To repeat it once more: Adolescence is no longer a well-defined period of transition with the task of preparing people for adulthood. Rather, adolescence has become a period of life in its own right. It has extended toward childhood and toward adulthood, thus turning into a protracted span of ten, fifteen, or even twenty years. Adolescence has become an ill-defined age with no clear beginning and without a clear end. This expansion and vagueness of adolescence has important educational implications. Obviously, adolescence is no longer a time for clear-cut decisions that will then provide a permanent basis for a further course of the life cycle called adulthood. This kind of fixed basis has become a logical impossibility because so many further changes are demanded of most people long after the time of traditional adolescence. Given this situation, it hardly makes sense anymore to look at adolescence as the fulcrum of human development as did the classic theorists of modern adolescence. And furthermore, this general view and reevaluation of the meaning of adolescence for the life cycle

as a whole have implications for our understanding of religious development as well. Once adolescence has ceased to be the one decisive transformational period that determines the future course of life, it also becomes doubtful if adolescence can still be expected to be the pivot of religious development. Instead, adolescence comes to be seen just like the other stages in the life cycle—as a period with special needs and with special possibilities but not as the one exceptional time for claiming or creating one's faith for the remainder of one's life.

A good example for how this changing understanding of the position of adolescence in religious development affects Christian education may be found with the contemporary discussion on confirmation.[48] In many cases, the model of the religious oath that was introduced in early modernity as a threshold on the way to mature or adult faith has been abandoned. Confirmation is no longer considered the occasion for professing a lifetime decision for the Christian faith. These traditional expectations and rites are now often seen as contradicting the realities of adolescent life and faith. Instead, educators and ministers emphasize that the church or congregation should stay in touch with the adolescents, accompanying them on their religious journeys—with their ups and downs and including the doubtful and searching questions that many adolescents have in mind and that often do not appear to be particularly Christian. The changing ways of doing confirmation are more than an arbitrary example. Rather, thinking of confirmation not as a fixed ritual tradition but as a task that may be carried out in different ways depending on the situation and on the context of young people's life styles points to the specific character of this first task of church and theology vis-à-vis postmodern youth, that is, becoming open and flexible enough to adapt educational programs to the challenges posed by the changing face of contemporary adolescence.

Of course, confirmation is not the only example, and suggesting new models for doing confirmation and confirmation class is not enough to respond to the needs of postmodern youth. For example, the long duration of adolescence also entails the emergence of new age groups that are not even in view as long as we just speak or think of adolescence as a single period in life. As mentioned before, at the upper end of adolescence there is now postadolescence (which we will discuss in chapter 4). And there are certain indications that another new age group is emerging at the beginning of adolescence as well. With adolescence starting earlier and earlier, childhood has become shorter and shorter. In many cases, childhood is seen as coextensive with the first decade of life. This seems to leave especially the ten- to twelve-year-olds in some kind of limbo. Traditionally the ten- to twelve-year-olds used to be treated as children, but they have clearly ceased to be children in the traditional sense. And although some of the habits that they have assumed move them closer to the adolescents, they still are not the same as, say, the sixteen- or eighteen-year-olds. There still is no special name for the time between ten and twelve years of age (if we exclude the traditional noncommittal and not very informative designation of "early adolescence," which avoids giving this age span a name of its own).[49] Yet the attention given to this age group among those in feminist psychology[50] has increased markedly, which may be taken as a first step in this direction.

Such changes, which lead to the emergence of several distinct age groups within adolescence itself, also raise important questions for religious education and youth ministry. Assuming that different groups require different offerings, the question must be raised: Do the traditional structures of Christian education, youth ministry, or other congregational programs still fit the changing structure of the age groups? Programs, for example, that are advertised "for children" are no longer attractive to eleven-year-olds who do not want to be children. And the traditional programs developed for fifteen- to sixteen-year-olds are not exactly thrilling for twenty-five-year-old postadolescents.

According to my own observations, churches have been rather slow in adapting their programs to the demands of changing or newly emerging age groups. There is no reason, however, why we should not at least try out some new ways that are more in line with postmodern expectations, identities, and forms of life. The Christian faith certainly does not depend on holding on to program structures that were developed for a traditional modern situation and that may not fit today's needs any more. It should become an ongoing task of Christian education and youth ministry to check, at least periodically, what the changing shape of adolescence may mean in terms of structuring their work and addressing different target groups. Christian youth work cannot be isolated from the general situation of youth. Unfortunately, this is often overlooked, probably because of today's very specialized approaches, which tend to focus on faith and religion in adolescence while neglecting the wider context of adolescent life and existence in general.

(2) The second task for theology and the church that I want to describe here refers to the growing tension—or even division—between the *church* and *individual religion or spirituality*.[51] How can we express

the Christian tradition in such a way that adolescents will experience this tradition not as boring, dated, and out of touch with their own reality, but rather as helpful, supportive, and truly challenging? From my perspective, a new and different understanding of theological correlation could be of help in this respect.

When I refer to theological correlation I do not want readers to adopt a particular type of theology like, for example, David Tracy's so-called revisionist theology with his attempt of bringing the Christian tradition and contemporary experiences into a mutually critical dialogue.[52] The task that I have in mind is much broader than the particular approach a single theologian can express. I consider theological correlation to refer to the general process of reconnecting the Christian tradition with the context of contemporary life. If what many of today's theologians and religious educators say is true, that one of the foundational tasks of contemporary theology consists of a correlative effort of bringing tradition and contemporary situations into a critical and constructive dialogue with each other,[53] then we will have to learn to address not only human experience in general but the specific postmodern situation and the specific experiences of today's adolescents. In my understanding, this includes a whole new way of doing theology. Traditionally, theology has devoted its utmost care to the study of its sources in Bible, tradition, and history; today, theology must learn how to study the worlds of contemporary adolescents with similar effort and care. What do we really know about the longings and hopes of young people? Are we able to describe their ethical standards, not in the judgmental ways of adults whose standards supposedly are superior, but in a way that is understandable as well as acceptable to the adolescents themselves? For example, it was quite striking to me how teenagers whom we included in a recent interview study spoke of their wish of becoming "good persons."[54] I was not only surprised that representatives of the so-called hedonist generation would express a goal for themselves that is so clearly not egotistic or self-centered but was even more surprised how deeply they seem to feel about this goal as an overall direction for their personal lives.

Educators have always known that adolescents tend to be misjudged and underestimated by adults. Some have even gone as far as pleading for educators to become advocates in defense of youth. So the observations from current interviews with youth are nothing new. What is new, however, is the demand that correlational theology must go beyond the very general and abstract reference to "human experiences" or to "contemporary life" in general. To say it once more: Theology's attempt to come into conversation with the experiences and lives of adolescents must be based on a careful analysis of their interests, outlooks, longings, and desires. As long as we have not made the serious and prolonged attempt of putting ourselves into the position of today's adolescents and of seeing the world as they do, we have not fulfilled our task as theologians or Christian educators. In any case, we have not made the effort of truly correlating their world to the Christian tradition.

To put it differently, the cleavage between the church and individual religion or spirituality can only be closed, or can at least become smaller, to the degree that adolescents can come to realize that what they associate with spirituality can be quite close to what the Christian tradition really is about, that is, the search for a meaningful life based on answers to the big questions—for example, of life and death or of the origin and future of this world. And this in turn presupposes that theology and the church acquire a new type of literacy in terms of adolescent life and experience. To come back to the example mentioned above: If today's adolescents are still longing to become "good persons," ministers and educators need to be able to offer them a vision of the good person that is based on the Christian tradition and that still makes sense to them vis-à-vis their views of contemporary moral life and of society. Or, to mention another example, adolescents' concerns about the future—their own personal future as well as the future of society—include much more than issues of technology or politics. Often, there is a religious dimension to such concerns in that they are related to far-reaching questions of apocalypticism or eschatology, of the end of time and of human finitude, of responsibility beyond one's lifetime, and so forth.[55]

Doing theology by facing up to such questions, feelings, experiences, and sometimes diffuse longings is not an easy task. Textbook knowledge will only carry us so far with this task. And many theologians and educators will rightly feel that they have not been trained to do this kind of theologizing. Yet, unless we come to be true partners in dialogue for today's adolescents, including the questions for which we have no ready-made answers (why does evil exist?) or for which we may even be lacking an adequate language, the gap between the church and personal religion or spirituality will only become wider and wider. My next two points may illustrate further what this means for the work of theology and Christian education.

(3) The third task that church and theology have to face refers to the experience of *pluralization*, especially the pluralization of *truth*

claims and of *religious orientations.* If we want to enable adolescents to move beyond the state of relativism and of agnostic tolerance, we will have to change our traditional ways of introducing them to the Christian tradition. It is not enough anymore to introduce them to one tradition, even if we approach this task, as we should, with the utmost care and with the most advanced teaching methods. As long as adolescents will encounter different—if not outright contradictory— points of view as soon as they listen to the media or as soon as they encounter the wider public, we will have to prepare them for this situation. In my understanding, the only way of doing this consists of including the question of how Christian convictions compare with those of other religions or worldviews and to consider together with them the conflicting truth claims that are part of the experience of plurality. I am not arguing for a so-called multifaith approach to religious education or for a neutral teaching based on religious studies, which aims at only informing students *about* religion in general. It is for the sake of Christian education that we need to address other truth claims and convictions.

If adolescents gain the impression that Christian education and youth ministry are exclusively focused on the Christian faith and that other convictions are not even taken into consideration, there is nothing to prevent them from feeling that the basis of what they have been offered is quite arbitrary. It must, in fact, appear arbitrary as long as it is not made clear why the Christian perspective should be preferable to other perspectives. In today's situation, they will inevitably become aware of other convictions and worldviews, and this is why they need to know how to consider them from a Christian point of view. If Christian education does not include such considerations, it leaves the adolescents unprepared for the experience of plurality, thus putting an intellectual burden upon them that they cannot handle.

(4) Finally, the experience of the *plural self* and of *plural identities* must be *evaluated theologically.* Is the pluralization of the self a process that should be appreciated by theology and should be acclaimed and supported by Christian education and youth ministry? Or, should it be the aim of theology to design a path that could lead back to a unitary self?

This question is not only of theoretical importance. Rather, at least some of the adolescents themselves seem to suffer from the ambiguity of not having a clear-cut identity and therefore are actively looking for an escape from plurality. In the context of fundamentalism, this process has been described in some detail.[56] Plurality may produce strong feelings of insecurity and disorientation and consequently may lead to the adherence to fundamentalist beliefs, which promise to put an end to all irritating questions.

In the light of such experiences, I want to close this chapter with three exemplary considerations on how a theological perspective on the self may help in coming to terms with plurality without taking flight into fundamentalism.

First, the experience of the plural self may be seen in relation to the Christian doctrine of justification by faith, which was first developed by Martin Luther on a biblical basis.[57] In terms of theological anthropology, this doctrine leads to the understanding that human identity cannot adequately be interpreted as human achievement. The identity of a person is not the product solely of the person's actions, even if it cannot be separated from these actions. The human person is always more than what the person does and achieves—the person is and remains God's creature. In reference to identity, this means that true identity is grounded in the relationship to God. It is relational not in the sense that it can, should, or must enter relationships, but in the sense that it is, in fact, a relationship that constitutes this identity at its most foundational level. This understanding is shared by many theologians, who emphasize the transcendent basis of human selfhood and who continue by pointing out that, from a Christian perspective, relationality is a core characteristic of the human being.[58] But what does this mean in the context of postmodernity and of postmodern adolescence?

In order to answer this question, we have to take this basic argument one step further in order to apply it to the experience of the plural self. By doing this, we come to realize that plurality and relationality are interconnected. The relational character of self and identity obviously contradicts all individualistic views of human existence. A relational self is never unitary in the sense of being centered exclusively in the human person itself. This is why the notion of a plural self can be helpful for realizing the importance of the relational character of the self, which is central to the Christian understanding. Another consequence concerns the achievement character of the unified self. If the human person is never responsible for his or her identity because, ultimately, this identity may only be received as a gift from God, this insight may actually help the self to carry the burden of its plural character. To put it differently, seeing identity as a gift may free us from being overly focused on how we ourselves can achieve its unity and completion. Instead, the idea of human completion itself becomes subject to a theological critique of ideology. The person in charge of his or her identity is trying to turn God's work into a human achievement.

The second consideration in theologically evaluating the pluralization of self and identity has again to do with justification by faith. The self or identity that conforms to the experience of being justified by faith has been described as a fragmentary self. The German theologian Henning Luther argues that the ability to accept oneself as a permanent fragment that never arrives at wholeness or completion is a direct consequence of the faith in God and in God's justifying love.[59] If this creative love is accepted as the truth of human existence, people can become free from the perfectionism that literally may drive them to death. If we take this understanding somewhat further, we can see that, from the beginning, the normative vision of theological anthropology is not an identity in perfect harmony with itself and with its aspirations. Rather, the expectation is the imperfect and therefore always fragmentary reality of life—with all its shortcomings, tensions, and unfulfilled longings. Of course, there also is the danger of idealizing the broken nature of human life. Praising the fragments should not make us forget the hope in God's power of healing. Yet healing does not mean that the fragments are just left behind and discarded; it means that they will be used in the process of healing. So without idealizing human existence in its fragmentary character, the notion of a fragmentary self can help us in evaluating— realistically as well as critically—the experience of the plural self. From a Christian point of view, the human self does not have to reach perfect unity but is allowed to remain fragmentary. But *fragmentary* does not mean ultimately *fragmented* in the sense of discontinuity and incoherence only. Relationality requires a fragmentary (imperfect) self because the perfect self does not need relationships. A fragmented self, however, is not able to carry on with any responsible relationship because this would require exactly the kind of continuity and coherence that it is lacking.

A final theological consideration carries this positive and critical view of pluralization even further. It also concerns the relationship between God and the plural self. From the point of view of the so-called new pneumatology, the experience of the plural self may be understood in relationship to God's liberating influence on human life, which frees the human person from the restrictions of having to conform to a narrowly defined individualistic identity.[60] According to this understanding, we may say that the self that is being transformed by the Spirit no longer has to strive for a self-centered and unitary identity. Rather, its very principle becomes openness—for God and for the richness of God's creation. But we also have to see that this openness is not to be confused with unlimited plurality. The openness of the Spirit is connected to the Christian faith. Therefore, it is a principled openness. There are principles or criteria by which to judge different options—principles of love and compassion, to mention only two of them.

More must be said about theological views of the postmodern life cycle. In chapter 7, I will come back to such questions as part of what I call a theology of the life cycle. Our task as Christian educators, youth ministers, and theologians is to lead children and youth on their path of understanding that the many options are not everything there is but that the search for what is true and what is good is still meaningful and necessary—even in the times of postmodernity.

CHAPTER 4

Religious Affiliation and Distancing in Postadolescence

The Impact of a Neglected Period of Life

In this chapter, I want to address a stage of the life cycle that is different from the ones considered in the previous chapters because it is a completely new stage of life. It was only about thirty years ago that the first references to "postadolescence" emerged in the literature.[1] At that time, social scientists observed that the transition between adolescence and adulthood was becoming more and more extended and that there was no more reason to speak of a transition rather than of a life-cycle stage of its own. The term "postadolescence" was introduced to denote what until then had been called late adolescence and/or early adulthood. It refers roughly to the third decade of life, but sometimes postadolescence is seen as starting at the age of eighteen or nineteen and as ending before or after one's thirtieth birthday. So again, there are no clear age limits. Postadolescence means a status– the status of no longer being an adolescent but of not yet having entered adulthood.

The first reason for including postadolescence in this study has to do with its relative newness. Due to its recent emergence, postadolescence can be seen as closely related to the contemporary changes of the life cycle that are the focus of the present study. The second reason for my interest in postadolescence has to do with its implications for religious development and religious education, which have not been sufficiently explored. As will be shown, postadolescence seems to be a time of crucial importance for religious affiliation and disaffiliation or distancing. Consequently, it deserves much more attention than it has generally received.

Unlike the periods of childhood and adolescence for which I could use traditional modern descriptions, there is no such description for postadolescence. Erik Erikson's model of the life cycle, which has been so helpful as a backdrop so far, does not foresee this stage of life. Some of what he says about late adolescence and early adulthood will still be useful in this chapter, but it cannot be used for a direct comparison between modern and postmodern understandings, that is, in the same way that I used it for the approach that I took in the chapters on childhood and adolescence. This is why I will proceed in a different manner in this chapter. My main interest is to make clear the challenges that postadolescence holds for theology and the church. In this sense, I take postadolescence as another example for the religious demands of postmodern life. In addition to this, I will discuss various explanations that have been offered for the religious changes taking place in late adolescence and early adulthood so that this chapter also offers some insights on different views of the life cycle and their practical consequences.

Religious Changes in Postadolescence: Empirical Observations

Empirical research on church members' attitudes toward the church has shown that these attitudes change markedly during late adolescence or early adulthood. If one attempts to characterize the typical person who is likely to drop his or her church membership, the factor of age appears to be one of the most prominent characteristics. It is some time during the third decade of life that dropping out most often occurs or is at least considered a possible choice. In addition to this, the general attitude toward being involved with the church—participating in its activities, adhering to its doctrines, considering the church as a valuable and important institution—also seems to become more distanced or negative.

Although these changes in late adolescence and early adulthood have been observed repeatedly and in different countries, the social and psychological reasons for these changes have rarely received special attention. Most often, two competing and rather general explanations are suggested. High dropout rates at this age are either taken as further evidence for the effects of secularization, or they are interpreted in terms of a life-cycle effect, which entails distance from the church in adolescence and a return to the church in later life. While both of these explanations will have to be considered in the following discussion, a simple choice between secularization and life-cycle effects may turn out to be all too simple. As will be shown, additional aspects and more refined perspectives have to be taken into account if we want to do justice to the religious changes in late adolescence and early adulthood.

The question of how to understand these changes is also of great interest to religious education, or at least it should be. Actually, there has rarely been a real focus on the religious education of this age group, which falls neither into the established category of youth work nor into that of adult education. Yet it is easy to see that, given the religious changes in this period of life, it may be of decisive importance to widen the horizon of religious education to include the period after the age of eighteen or twenty.

Moreover, the two explanatory approaches—secularization and life-cycle effects—are not very helpful for education. The expectation of a large-scale secularization of society is not encouraging for educational programs. Rather, against this background, such programs tend to be seen as hopelessly naïve and, in any case, without a real chance against the general societal process. But the life-cycle perspective also has its shortcomings in terms of education. Here, education may not be without a chance, but it certainly is not needed. If people come back to the church automatically once they get older, there is no real need to bring about this result through additional efforts. In the following discussion, I will first review some of the empirical data on religious attitudes in late adolescence and young adulthood, mostly in Germany (where I live and work) but also with an eye on the United States and some other countries as well. In a second section, which will be the main body of this chapter, I will describe and discuss a number of psychological and sociological interpretations that go beyond the simple opposition of secularization versus life-cycle effects. The final section will address the possible benefits of such interpretations for a more adequate understanding of our contemporary religious situation, as well as for religious education or youth ministry in late adolescence and young adulthood.

In several countries of the Western world, the eighteen- to thirty-year-old age group features prominently among the typical dropouts from the church. The situation in West Germany, for example, clearly shows this pattern. The three major surveys on church membership carried out for the Evangelical Church of Germany in the 1970s, the 1980s, and the 1990s consistently brought this result. Typical dropouts are young, unmarried professionals living in an urban environment[2]—a result that is corroborated by other studies.[3] For the United States, Wade Clark Roof and William McKinney report strikingly similar results: "Those who become nonaffiliates are young, predominatly male, well educated, more committed to alternative lifestyles, and oriented generally to an ethic of personal growth and self-fulfillment."[4] The situation in Switzerland, to mention another example, is especially noteworthy in regard to age. The percentage of Swiss persons without religious affiliation doubles from the second to the third decade of life, from approximately 5 to 10 percent and more.[5] All these studies show a similar picture: The typical dropout is never characterized by age alone. Yet in the different countries, age does play an important role, and it always is late adolescence or early adulthood that correlates with high dropout rates.

Leaving the church is only one indicator of distance from the church. Attitudinal as well as behavioral changes may also be found with those who stay members, for example, in their views of the church and in their forms of participation. Again, the German studies on church membership offer plenty of empirical evidence for such changes in late adolescence and young adulthood, and so does the more general research on youth.[6] In either case, there are clear changes in the sense of a growing distance from the church starting in middle or late adolescence. There is a clear decline in church attendance, and the feeling of being connected to the church weakens.

It is interesting to note that even in former East Block countries like East Germany, religious changes can be observed at this age. Of course, most of all, the atheist education of the former socialist state has left its mark on the religious attitudes of people there. So even today, the degree of religious affiliation is much lower in East Germany.[7] Yet with all the obvious differences between East and West Germany, the age group of the twenty- to thirty-year-olds still seems to play a special role in the East.[8] Today the highest rates of nonaffiliation are found in the age groups between eighteen and fifty-nine. Yet leaving the church most often occurred at the age of late adolescence and young adulthood.

Summarizing the empirical observations, one may say that late adolescence and early adulthood—or, to use the new designation, postadolescence—obviously play a major role in processes of religious distancing and disaffiliation. Clearly, it is never age alone that explains such effects. Nevertheless, age seems important enough to motivate a closer look at different possibilities of understanding the relationship between postadolescence as a new stage of the life cycle and the religious changes mentioned above.

Religious Change in Postadolescence: Possible Explanations

In this section, I will attempt to develop a more multifaceted and refined understanding of possible reasons for the religious changes observed in late adolescence and early adulthood. Given the focus of the present study on challenges for theology and the church, my considerations will be geared not to religion in general but mostly to Christian religion in a Western sense. It should be noted, however, that a similar attempt has been made by psychologists in Israel with a focus on Jewish (post)adolescents and on their ways of abandoning their religious affiliations and practices. While some of the factors described by the researchers in Israel, for example the Holocaust, have no immediate parallel in other countries, religions, or cultures (even if the Holocaust may also have influenced attitudes toward the Christian churches in other countries and especially in Germany), their general considerations of different factors involved in the distancing process show clear parallels to my own considerations concerning postadolescence in a Christian context.[9] Such parallels between the experiences in different religious contexts are another indicator for the importance of the effects connected to postadolescence.

The aspects or factors that I will suggest and discuss in the following section are meant to prepare the way for a clearer understanding of theoretical alternatives and of possible explanations. All of them have some empirical backing in existing studies on postadolescence, religion, and religious affiliation. Yet the existing data do not allow for a final assessment of the respective weight or influence of the various factors and of the validity of the competing explanations. I hope that greater conceptual clarity will help toward a clearer understanding of the challenges involved for church and theology.

Which aspects or factors are to be discussed here? In the introductory section of this chapter, two aspects to be considered have already been mentioned: secularization and effects within the life cycle. In addition to these, I will refer to developmental psychology, biography, cohort experience, historical periods, and to changes of the life cycle itself.

Progressive Secularization

It has often been argued that the decline of religious affiliation found in late adolescence and early adulthood indicates the progressive impact of secularization. If adults show, for example, consistently higher rates for church attendance, secularization theory leads to the prediction that today's adolescents will never reach such rates even as they get older. It is expected that the younger generation will always be more secular than the older generation. This view can also be supported with empirical results that indicate, for example, a marked and steady decline of religious education in childhood. If the members of different age groups are asked about the religious education that they received during childhood, the results indicate this decline to be a typical twentieth-century experience.[10]

Yet as plausible as some of the interpretations in terms of secularization may sound, there can be no doubt that some of the corresponding predictions even from twenty or thirty years ago have not held true. No one would want to claim that the American or German adolescents of twenty years ago have turned into exclusively secular adults in the present. Rather, quite in line with the general critique of the assumptions of secularization theory mentioned in chapter 1, their religious outlooks and attitudes may be considered as indicative of religious pluralization and individualization. Longitudinal studies, which would trace individual religious biographies from adolescence into middle and late adulthood, are not available. Cross-sectional data, for example in Germany, indicate that adolescents' relationships to the church have tended to become more tenuous over the last two decades, but their interest in religion has stayed the same or has even become stronger.[11]

While effects of secularization may certainly play a role for the religious experience in late adolescence and early adulthood in terms of institutions such as schools, universities, and business enterprises that have become more secular, for example, the concept of secularization in the sense of an overall decline of religion clearly is insufficient vis-à-vis the religious complexity of the contemporary situation of individual life as well as of social life.

Effects within the Life Cycle

The religious differences between postadolescence, with its distance to the church on the one hand, and later adulthood, with its higher rate of involvement with the church on the other, may also be seen as expressive of the typical breaking away from childhood beliefs and from parental identifications. I call this "effects within the life cycle" because such a breaking away and later coming back to the church fit well with the traditional model of the life cycle. Erikson, our main witness for the traditional (modern) expectations, often refers to the phenomenon of a "moratorium" needed by adolescents before they are ready to take over adult obligations and to make responsible choices concerning, for example, their professional training.[12] This idea of a moratorium can also be applied to religious development. It then entails the expectation that adolescents become more distant to, or even leave, the church, but that they will be ready to come back in adulthood. The moratorium is not permanent. It is an interlude that may last for many months or even years. But as people get older and as they move into proper adulthood, the experimental attitudes of the moratorium stay behind.

From this perspective, the higher rates on church-related indicators to be found with older age groups are seen as the future of today's adolescents. After they move out of their moratorium, they are expected to show the same degree of religious affiliation as their parents' generation does.

While explanations based on secularization and on life-cycle effects are sometimes treated as alternatives that mutually exclude each other, they actually can also go together,[13] so that tendencies of secularization are spurred by psychologically sensitive periods in life, and so that, conversely, certain parts of the life cycle receive new meaning and result in a different outcome because of progressive secularization. Again, in the absence of longitudinal data, it remains difficult to determine if the expected life-cycle effects are still operative today and if they can be expected to bring today's young people back to the church in the future. Yet given the high rate of cultural change that is typical for postmodernity, it seems unlikely that the human life cycle operates as a fixed pattern and that it will not be affected by changing circumstances. This is why I will consider in the following pages effects not only *within* the life cycle but also effects related to changes *of* the life cycle itself, the main perspective of my own approach.

Effects of Cognitive Development

Sometimes life-cycle effects and developmental effects are taken to mean the same. For the traditional type of developmental psychology, which assumed that all developments mainly depended on age, this was certainly true. Yet, for the more recent understanding of development, we have to distinguish clearly between age and developmental achievements. While a given age may often be the statistical presupposition for a certain developmental level, no such level can be predicted from age alone. Lawrence Kohlberg's well-known stages of moral judgment are a good example for this.[14] The so-called postconventional moral stages, which are characterized by independent moral reasoning based on general ethical principles, are not found before early adulthood. Yet many people at this age have not reached these stages. Rather, their moral judgement level is conventional, that is, based on the views of a certain group or society rather than on general principles, and it may stay conventional for most or all of their lives. This is why age or the stage of the life cycle does not allow for predictions of the development achieved.

If we distinguish in this way between the life cycle, through which, inevitably, everyone has to go, and cognitive, moral, or religious development, which, for the respective level achieved, is dependent on influences of the environment, we may also gain additional insights into the changes in late adolescence and early adulthood. The research on cognitive and moral development as well as on religious development points out that this age may bring about highly critical as well as strongly individualizing conceptions of truth and of religious meaning.[15] In this view, it is a powerful new cognitive capacity that makes traditional religious convictions appear naïve and questionable. As a respondent at the age of approximately twenty years puts it in his statement, the idea of God has been "created by humans and for humans…in order to summarize certain value orientations." But with the "progress in the development of humankind on the level of the humanities as well as of natural science, the naïve constructions of value transmission lose their meaning."[16] This young person sounds like a nineteenth-century philosopher, and this is no coincidence. The newly acquired cognitive capacity of looking "behind" traditional ideas makes people at this stage suspicious of their truth. They tend to rely much more on their own reasoning than on the group or congregation, to which they may still belong. But even if they still belong to a congregation, their religious outlooks clearly have a distancing effect in that they will find it difficult, if not impossible, to accept a given faith without deeply questioning it.

To my knowledge, the relationship between religious development and religious (dis)affiliation in late adolescence and early adulthood has not been given attention in the research on church membership or on dropouts. Yet the questions to be asked seem obvious: Does a certain level of cognitive, moral, or religious development correlate with distance from the church and with religious disaffiliation? And concerning the further course of religious development: Is there any indication that something like a later reversal may occur—a reappraisal of the church that accompanies a different developmental level, for example, James W. Fowler's "conjunctive faith" stage, which is sometimes characterized as "second naïveté" in the sense of a return to the earlier appreciation for symbol, story, and ritual *after* having gone through a time of critically rejecting them?[17]

The relationship between religious disaffiliation and religious development also points to education as another possible factor involved. In various countries, the distancing effects of a high level of education have been observed in people's attitudes toward the church.[18] Other psychologists observe that education seems to stimulate religious development.[19] But what exactly is the relationship among all three factors—education, religious disaffiliation, and religious development? Are there typical patterns to be described, for example, in terms of certain stages? What kind of education might support a religious reappraisal?

Biographical Influences

In this context, the term "biographical" is not used in the sense of the life cycle. Rather, it refers to the coincidental events and changes that characterize a certain person's course of life—for example, time and place of birth, time of marriage, professional choices, and so forth. To some degree, such events and changes are not limited to the individual course of life but are roughly the same for many people, at least at a given time in history. There are typical ages for marriage, typical kinds of education, typical professional careers. In this perspective, biographies are not only individual but are also standardized, because they exhibit typical characteristics.

For late adolescence and early adulthood, a number of such typical biographical situations clearly play a role in the present context. Often late adolescence is the time when young people move away from their parents. They go to college or to university, or they find themselves a job that gives them financial independence.

While it is clear that these aspects contribute to the special character of late adolescence and young adulthood, it is not obvious how they are related to religious attitudes. Not enough empirical research has been done on these aspects. A study on the religious orientations of university students carried out in Germany shows that the majority of the students perceive a great distance between themselves and the church.[20] Nevertheless, many of them indicate that they are interested in religion. It seems that the independence that they claim for their lives carries over to their religious attitudes, and this makes them critical of the church and of religious institutions in general. In their eyes, institutionalized religion does not support religious autonomy but demands acceptance of fixed teachings and of the rules that are set by the institutions without allowing for much influence from the individual believers.

Generational and Cohort-specific Aspects

The two terms "generation" and "cohort" are used interchangeably here. In the present context, the reference to "generations" or "cohorts" is important in that it directs attention to the educational process that always takes place between two or more generations or age groups.

The educating (adult) generation or cohort is always influenced by certain experiences that were typically present at the time of their being shaped in childhood and adolescence, as well as in later adulthood. When the empirical reference to late adolescence and early adulthood as special times of religious disaffiliation was first established in the 1970s and 1980s, the corresponding studies actually referred not to adolescence in general.[21] Rather, they referred to a specific cohort that was largely influenced by the cultural and political changes of the 1960s. In several studies and for different countries, the time of the 1960s was characterized as the watershed of postwar religious culture.[22] After 1945 and until the 1960s, a conservative alignment of the nation state, public authority, church, and religion prevailed in many Western countries. With the changes of the 1960s, this alignment dissolved and, consequently, different attitudes became dominant that were critical of all authority and tradition, including the church. It is well known that the younger generation was the main carrier of the new culture of the 1960s.

Another implication of the generational background of religious disaffiliation in the 1970s, which has received much less attention in research, concerns the role of the members of the so-called baby boom generation as educators. Roof has portrayed this generation in the 1990s as a "generation of seekers."[23] According to his results, the members of this cohort are not areligious or antireligious. Yet only some of them have found a way back into the traditional mainstream churches. If we take such observations one step further, we arrive at the hypothesis that this generation will also have exerted a corresponding educational influence on their children who, in many cases, are in late adolescence and early adulthood today. If this is true, the specific experience of the 1960s must be considered as an important background for the empirical findings on religious changes in late adolescence and young adulthood, not only in their immediate impact on young people in the 1960s and 1970s but also on those who have been raised by mothers and fathers of that generation in later years.

This understanding—that the religious disaffiliation to be observed in late adolescence and early adulthood may not be a sign of a general breakdown of family religious education in the sense of secularization but rather is indicative of a certain style and orientation within the contemporary family—can be supported further by empirical studies from Germany where the processes mentioned above are especially salient. A study looking into three different generations within families, for example, clearly showed that families may be successful in passing on religious orientations even if such orientations strongly differ from the church's expectations.[24] What is perceived as a decline of religion from the perspective of the church can, at the same time, accordingly mean success for the families. Similarly, and against widespread expectations, the most recent survey on childhood in Germany supports the view that the family is very successful in handing on religious traditions to the next generation, much more so than in many other respects, such as musical interests or sports.[25] The religion handed on by the family, however, often is not identical with what the church expects or teaches. Rather, it is a highly individualized type of religion, which is closely related to family life, to biographical patterns, to crisis experiences within the family, or just to the general needs experienced by the family.

Changing Historical Periods

The notions of generation and cohort that I introduced in the preceding section are based on the idea that society and culture are in constant flux, an idea that is especially plausible for the modern or postmodern situation with its rapid rate of change and its many innovations, for example, in the fields of technology and the media. What is referred to in the title of this subsection as "changing historical periods" takes this idea even further. There is not only the continuous flux of cultural change, but there are also sharp turns and breaks or breakdowns that may no longer be adequately described by metaphors of steady continuity.

One of the most clear-cut recent examples of such turns and breakdowns in the Western world can be found in the events of 1989, which put an end to the former East Block governments and sometimes even to the respective states themselves. The German unification in 1990, for example, which was part of this process, clearly changed the religious situation. While there was a palpable increase in the degree of young adults' closeness to the church in former East

Germany between 1991 and 1994, the general level of religious affiliation in that part of the country has stayed very low, bringing down the figures for church membership in Germany as a whole to about 70 percent.[26] Consequently, the general religious climate in Germany is quite different from what it used to be in West Germany before 1990.

Examples of changing historical periods and of their impact on religious attitudes may be found at earlier times as well. A well-known case, again from Germany, is the end of National Socialism and of its antichurch politics in 1945. In this case, a considerable number of dropouts from the church resumed their former membership.

The experience of sudden historical changes and of the breakdown of political systems or ideologies is most likely of lasting influence within the biographies of the people. In addition to this, it may be hypothesized that late adolescence and young adulthood are times in life that are especially sensitive to such influences. Long-term studies with those who were at this age in 1989–1990 may shed some more light on the interplay between historical, cohort, and life-cycle effects, just as in the case of the adolescents and young adults of the 1960s mentioned above. And as I am writing this, people are wondering what September 11, 2001, will mean for the religious biographies of our contemporaries.

The Changing Face of the Life Cycle

With this perspective, we come back to the central focus of my own approach, which reckons not only with changes *within* the life cycle but also with changes *of* the life cycle itself. In other words, if we take seriously that the life cycle itself is not an anthropological given but is subject to far-reaching changes, we have to ask if and how the processes of religious disaffiliation in late adolescence and early adulthood can be explained by changes of the life cycle. The term "postadolescence" suggests that a new stage of life has emerged between adolescence and adulthood. If this is true, we have to wonder if the church has kept pace with the needs and interests of this new stage. If we assume, at least hypothetically, that postadolescence has become a reality for many young people, it follows that the traditional programs offered for adolescents on the one hand and for adults on the other will no longer be attractive for those who have left behind adolescence but have not entered adulthood.

Even if I cannot draw on empirical data about what congregations offer for postadolescents, it seems fair to say that, on the whole, church-related programs have been very slow to meet the needs and interests of this new age group. So it may be argued that distance from the church in this case is not due to young people's lack of interest in religion, but rather to the absence of attractive possibilities for their participation.

In the next section of this chapter, I will presuppose this hypothesis by making it the starting point for my considerations of constructive responses by church and theology.

Facing Up to Postadolescence: How the Church Can Profit from Moving beyond Traditional Expectations

In this chapter, I have chosen an approach that is different from the one used in other chapters of this book. Following the interest in understanding the religious demands of postmodern life from the perspective of the postmodern life cycle, my focus was on the neglected religious importance of late adolescence and early adulthood. While empirical data from international research establish this importance beyond possible doubt, competing explanations for these observations are still under discussion. Yet, it is easy to see that the traditional assumptions of secularization theory are of limited help in finding such explanations. The same is true for expectations connected to traditional patterns within the life cycle that may not hold true anymore. Consequently, we have to reckon with possible changes of the life cycle itself in that a new stage—postadolescence—has come into the picture.

This observation is of great importance for our overall question concerning changes of the life cycle between modernity and postmodernity. The emergence of a new stage of the life cycle can be seen as strong evidence for the far-reaching changes that have actually occurred. And in addition to this, we can also see how attention to these changes may help the work of theology and the church. In the last section of this chapter, I want to consider in some more detail some of the constructive responses by which church and theology can address the challenges connected to postadolescence. Four aspects are of special importance.

(1) There is no reason for the church either to give up on this age group or to adapt the just-wait-and-see attitude that expects the postadolescents to return to the church in their adult years. These options correspond to the traditional opposition of secularization versus life-cycle effects, which has turned out to be much too superficial. Both concepts—the ideas of secularization and of the life cycle—are not fine-grained enough to catch and to render a reliable image of life in today's late adolescence and early adulthood. What

once appeared, from a traditionally modern perspective, as the progressive and steady decline of religion is more and more replaced by the multifaceted understanding of religious pluralization and individualization. And the same holds true for the life cycle. It has become much more difficult to derive fixed expectations from the traditional models of the life cycle. In this sense, we must move beyond the two typically modern expectations if we want to do justice to the religious changes occurring in late adolescence and early adulthood. They can be explained neither by secularization theory nor by classic models of the life cycle, which do not foresee a stage of postadolescence.

To put it positively: Reckoning with the possibility of postadolescence as a new stage can become an important impulse for addressing the special needs and interests of those who are in this stage. It can encourage church and theology to revise their expectations as well as the programs offered for them. But before looking into this possibility, we first have to address some additional presuppositions.

(2) Considering the possibility of postadolescence may help us in overcoming the vicious circle that is operative in the present situation of little to no contact between the church and people in late adolescence or early adulthood. This analysis may be more accurate for European countries than for the United States, where the emphasis on college ministry and on programs for young adults is stronger than in Europe. However, even in the United States, postadolescence is clearly less in view than childhood and (early) adolescence. Compared to offerings for children and younger adolescents, not many programs are trying to address postadolescents. Educators and ministers seem to assume that there is no real need. Often, they argue that having fewer programs for this age group corresponds directly to the lack of interest and openness of this group. Yet given the considerations above, one must wonder if this correlation between lacking programs and lacking interest should not also be read the other way around. In other words, interest may be lacking because no attractive programs are offered, which is what I consider a vicious circle: no programs and no expectations, no responses and no interest. The concept of postadolescence can help to stop this circle, because it forces us to rethink the traditional assumptions about this age group.

From this perspective, there is not only a need for new and additional efforts toward this age group but even more for specific efforts. Programs and activities must be designed specifically for them. But who are they? And what do we know about them?

(3) Characterizing postadolescents by stating that they are *no longer* adolescents and *not yet* adults amounts to a purely negative description. Just comparing them to what they are *not* leaves them in a state of limbo. Psychologists such as Erik Erikson or Daniel Levinson have stressed the issues of independence from the family of origin and of finding a career; others, for example Carol Gilligan, whose focus is more inclusive of women, emphasize the importance of intimacy and relationships.[27] Earlier accounts that specifically address postadolescence refer to the openness and experimental attitude to be observed with this age group.[28] Altogether, our knowledge about this time of life must be called very limited, especially compared to the bodies of research and literature on childhood or youth.

When we ask about religion in postadolescence, this is even more true. Existing research has generally neglected religion in late adolescence and young adulthood. In their broader accounts of faith development, theorists such as Fowler include references to this age group, but rarely have they made it their focal concern.[29] For example, Evelyn and James Whitehead focus on the relationship between "intimacy and religious growth" in young adulthood, but they do not offer a broad view of this stage, let alone the issue of postadolescence as a new stage of the life cycle.[30] The major study still is Sharon Parks's *The Critical Years,* in which she stresses the importance of faith development in young adulthood:

> The power and vulnerability of young adulthood lie in the experience of the dissolution and recomposition of the meaning of self and world and its challenges to faith. To become a young adult in faith is to discover the limits of one's assumptions about how "life will always be"–and to recompose a meaningful sense of self and world of the other side of that discovery.[31]

Parks's plea for more attention to these "critical years" has unfortunately not brought about a sustained interest in finding out more about the religious trajectories in the years between age twenty and thirty. Consequently, church and theology first of all must come to realize the importance of getting to know religion in postadolescence. What I said in the previous chapter concerning religion in adolescence is equally true in respect to postadolescence: Theology and the church must apply their utmost care to "reading," interpreting, and understanding the meaning structures of the life worlds of young people, no less than they are used to carefully reading the Christian sources. Otherwise, the distance between the church and the postadolescents will never be overcome.

(4) The final outcome of the new orientations vis-à-vis postadolescence must, of course, be concrete and practical. New and different
possibilities for young people to participate in the church must be
called into life. And most likely, the traditional congregation with its
programs will not do for this purpose because people in late
adolescence and early adulthood generally do not consider it to be
"their" place. The minimum to be done in this respect is to create
new spaces within existing congregations, spaces that are designed
for this age group and that clearly extend an invitation to them.

Beyond the congregation, other locations that are important in
the life of this age group also deserve more attention than they
generally receive in church and theology. College ministry is one
example, but we should also not lose sight of higher education as a
whole.[32] The type of rationality or the kind of career orientation taught
by colleges and universities is certainly one of the factors that make it
difficult for the students to recognize the need for a religious worldview
or ethics that can guide their individual lives as well as give direction
to the use of scientific knowledge in society.

Another context not to be overlooked by church and theology
involves the special interest groups and parareligious organizations
that can be quite attractive for young adults. Environmentalism, peace,
and worldwide justice are just some of the more well-known issues
taken up by such groups. And often these issues include a religious
or even clearly Christian dimension, such as the relationship between
ecology and creation, between political peace and the Christian vision
for peace, or between justice in the world and God's justice. In many
cases, however, the religious dimensions are not obvious for the young
people themselves, and, even more, they cannot see how church and
theology are addressing such issues. Consequently, there is a need
for church and theology to speak in such a way that postadolescents
can come to realize their potential contribution toward society's
commitment to a sustainable future.

In addition to this, there is a need for programs that directly
address the life situations and questions that are central to this stage
of the life cycle.[33] As mentioned above, these are issues of leaving
one's family of origin, of choosing a career, and of intimacy,
relationships, and marriage—and even, perhaps, divorce.[34] And they
also include a testing and reordering of the orientations one has found
for one's life and faith at earlier times.[35] So there are many topics that
could be taken up by church and theology. Why has this not been
done more in the past?

Two difficulties or even obstacles for theology and the church in
their attempt at reaching out more directly and effectively to

postadolescents must at least be mentioned in concluding this chapter. These difficulties concern theological and ecclesial challenges.

- *What is the place of the critical thinker in a congregation?* This question does not refer only to those who expect, for example, a sermon to be intellectually sound. Rather, it refers to an attitude of criticism or even of skepticism toward the Christian faith itself. Can theology and the church limit themselves to those who "have faith" and who are in agreement with the congregation? Shouldn't there be places, spaces, and opportunities for being critical and experimental about the faith without having to leave the church?

- *Can the church appreciate experimental lifestyles?* One characteristic of postadolescence is its openness for new possibilities and for lifestyles that are different from the parents' lives and from society's traditional expectations. At certain times in the past, for example in the 1960s, this amounted to a real counterculture; today, more moderate deviations can be expected—regarding food and clothes, entertainment and housing, media and cultural preferences, relationships and sexual orientations. The experimental lifestyles of postadolescence can clearly come into contradiction with what the adult members of the church consider acceptable. Yet if the church is to become more attractive for people going through postadolescence, we have to distinguish between what is theologically necessary and what is just customary in the church, thus making space for new and different ways in the church and discovering that postadolescent experimentation can become a learning field for the adults in the church as well.

CHAPTER 5

Church, Individual Religion, Public Responsibility

Images of Faith between Modern and Postmodern Adulthood

The preceding chapter on postadolescence made it necessary to take an approach that is in line with this new stage in the life cycle and that was therefore different from the approach used for childhood and adolescence in chapters 2 and 3. With the present chapter, we can return to the procedure established in the first three chapters, that is, we can confront the modern understanding of the life cycle, which now has become the traditional view, with those changes that are emerging today. Since this procedure will be of special importance in this chapter, it may be helpful to be reminded of the reasons behind this way of approaching adulthood.

I am interested in adulthood as part of what may be called the postmodern life cycle and in the contribution of practical theology to helping people lead their lives faithfully and responsibly under the conditions of postmodernity. Consequently, the first task may be seen as describing and understanding the position of adulthood in postmodernity, the second as offering guiding images of faith that are capable of addressing the demands of postmodern life.

Since it cannot be presupposed that the views of postmodernity offered by philosophical analyses also hold true empirically for contemporary forms of everyday life, a more inductive procedure is in place for practical theology. In any case, a more empirical approach is needed if practical theology is to address the demands of postmodern life as contemporary people actually experience them. This is why I will start by asking about the once modern understanding of adulthood, which now has become the traditional one. In a second step, my focus will be on the changes that may be observed when we compare modern adulthood with today's experiences and perceptions of adult life. After this, I will be in the position to ask, in a third step, how theology and the church may respond to the challenges that postmodern adulthood entails for them.

The Traditional Vision: The Modern Autonomous Individual

Modernity has been especially productive in terms of images of adulthood. This is why my focus in this section will be on such images. In some ways, we may say that modernity itself was closely connected with the proud hope that humankind had finally reached adulthood and maturity. In any case, the immature dependence of preenlightenment times was to be overcome. Kant's famous response to the question, "What is Enlightenment?" may be understood as a powerful image defining adulthood: leaving the state of being a dependent minor, leaving the state of not being autonomous.[1] In Kant's understanding, the lack of autonomy first of all referred to a lack of autonomous judgment—a state of not making use of one's rational capacities as a human person. *Sapere aude!*—Dare to know!—is the decisive step toward enlightenment.

On a more popular level, one might say that modernity stands for the equating of adulthood with autonomy, with independence, and with rationality. In this view, dependence is in turn identified with being a child who is still lacking autonomy, or with an elderly person who has lost his or her autonomy due to age or illness. Proper adulthood is then limited to that time of life in which one supposedly is in full possession of one's abilities and is therefore able to lead an autonomous life.

Another well-known image of adulthood was set forth by Sigmund Freud from the perspective of psychological health. For him, the ability to love and to work—*Lieben und Arbeiten*—characterizes the healthy adult.[2] And Freudian psychotherapy is aimed at restoring the ability to love and to work where it has been lost.

Erik Erikson, one of Freud's later followers in the United States (and our main source for the modern understanding of the life cycle), has reformulated the psychoanalytic understanding of adulthood. In his account of the human life cycle, Erikson uses the term "generativity" in order to describe the positive pole of adult development.[3] Generativity is a term that needs some explanation. From its Latin etymology, generativity points to the act of generating or producing something. It refers to the biological process of procreation but also to human work producing all kinds of artifacts. So with the notion of generativity, adulthood becomes identified with parenthood and with being part of the work force—or, in one of Erikson's more philosophical interpretations, with responsibility for the next generation in general and with creative work in all kinds of fields.[4]

In order fully to understand the image of generativity and its meaning for our visions of adulthood, we must also be aware of the way in which Erikson describes the negative pole that, as a constant threat, opposes generativity. This negative term is called "stagnation"— a term and image that allude to the state of being inactive and of not growing. In this sense, psychological stagnation may be compared with economic states of "no growth" that, in modernity, are not considered healthy and stable. In modern economics, "no growth" really means decline. In this view, the only healthy state is progress. So if the negative pole in adulthood is described as stagnation, the normative vision of being adult is based on the idea of progress— permanent progress and steady improvement.

What, then, is the modern vision of the truly adult person? If we combine the philosophical with the psychological view, we arrive at the image of an individual who is autonomous, independent, and rational, and, moreover, is dynamically increasing in his or her capacities. The dual focus on love and work translates into a pattern of family life on the one hand and of a professional career on the other. And clearly, it is the life of a man that fits this pattern in the first place. Today, it is easy to see that this vision leads to a highly ideological and one-sided view of adulthood. Yet before critically examining this view in more detail, let us turn to the role of religion in modern adulthood.

What happens to *religion* within the modern view of adulthood? Does this view include a place for mature adult faith? Leaving the state of being a dependent minor in Kant's sense also means claiming one's freedom from all traditional authorities. Such authorities are seen as jeopardizing human autonomy in that they are not based on reason but on tradition. In this understanding, religion and, specifically, the church are considered as prime examples of institutions whose claims are not bound to rational argument but only to faithful adherence. So from the beginning, it is hard to reconcile adulthood in the modern sense with church and religion. Religion is welcome where it supports rational autonomy, especially in the realm of ethics, but there clearly is no central place for religion in adulthood.

In the same vein, from a psychological and sociological point of view, religion becomes confined to the margins—it is limited to certain periods of the life cycle and to those areas of adult life that, for one reason or another, are not fully accessible to enlightenment. For the modern view of adulthood as it is incorporated in psychological models of the life cycle, religion is tied to the time *before* and *after* proper adulthood, that is, it is primarily identified with childhood and with old age. And even if religion is given a prominent place at the onset of adulthood—in adolescent development as it may also be found in Erikson's account of the life cycle[5]—it is only in such a way that religion may support the emergence of adulthood, but it is clearly not to define the meaning of adulthood. Rather, the location of religion in childhood and in old age goes along with a clear separation between secular life in public, which becomes the true arena of adult life, and religion as a private matter that is to be confined to one's heart and, possibly, is to be expressed in church as a private institution. According to this view, the church has its focus on children and on older people who have retired from working life, and it is addressing situations like illness and death, which are located on the fringes of modern rationality.

This observation leads to more general considerations concerning the role of religion and Christianity in modern society. Adulthood as the proper age and status of modern people has its prime location within the secular space of work and public life. The religion of the modern adult is a religion of inner personal feelings. It is accompanied by an ethics that may be motivated by a particular religion but that takes on a religiously neutral form. From a different perspective, one may also say that, with modernity, three different types of Christianity and religion have emerged: religion in the church, individual religion, and public religion, which often takes the form of civil religion, that is, of a religiously grounded morality that undergirds the public order but is not related to any particular religious community or tradition.[6] As we will see in the next section, these different types of religion also play a role in postmodernity.

Postmodern Challenges

The modern image of adulthood still plays an extremely powerful role in contemporary society, and many of us feel the hold that the image of becoming—and remaining—adults in the full sense of the word actually has on our deep sense of direction in life. Yet at the same time, it has also become more than obvious that the idea of modern adulthood captured above is an ideology that can hardly be used as a basis for one's life. It is an ideology in that it never included the life perspectives of those who may not expect a career—women who take care of children and families, for example, or the sick and handicapped who are not able to perform according to the standards of modern production. All of them are excluded from the status of being proper modern adults, just like elderly people who, according to this understanding, lose the normative status of progressive autonomy. And to the degree that human beings can never be only autonomous, all of them fail to measure up to this notion of adulthood.

Moreover, the modern image of adulthood is an ideology in that the normative ideals of autonomy, independence, rationality, and ever-dynamic progress are self-contradictory and detrimental. This is true in at least two respects. First, the normative expectations contradict each other. For example, the economic idea of progress does not necessarily lead to more personal autonomy. Rather, the economic systems are claiming independence from personal control—they have turned into impersonal and objective powers that clearly limit the influence of individual persons. And second, the four ideals—autonomy, independence, rationality, and progress—are paradoxical in that it is impossible to maximize them without destroying their meaning. As we have come to understand today, maximum economic progress does not mean maximum wealth. Often it only means the destruction of the natural presuppositions of the economy. Similarly, maximum autonomy of the person does not mean maximum freedom. Rather, it only means the destruction of the social relationships that all personal life needs as its basis.

Another critical point that has been raised against the traditional idea of modern adulthood concerns the image of the ideal course of life as a linear curve. This curve rises up from childhood or adolescence to reach its peak in midadulthood in order to then decline, slowly and softly, into a well-cushioned retirement. Empirical studies starting in the 1960s and 1970s have clearly shown a different picture. Take, for example, Daniel Levinson's account *The Seasons of a Man's Life* published in 1978, which later, in the 1990s, was extended to include *The Seasons of a Woman's Life.*[7] The picture of the "developmental periods in early and middle adulthood" that Levinson offers definitely is not a curve—although it still contains the remnants of the ideology of progress in that it looks like steps leading the person to ever higher levels of achievement.[8] Yet it is quite noticeable, even in this idealized picture, that the course of life is neither linear nor does it follow a steady movement in one or another direction. Rather, adulthood is now recognized as comprising many different crises and several turning points.

How would the picture look today if we ourselves would have to design one? I suppose there would not be many steps left. Rather, we would draw our lives with several lines simultaneously—different lines or strands that sometimes flow together but more often follow different directions: working life, private life, relationships, possibly memberships, spiritual journeys, and so forth. In sum, adulthood no longer is the time after the great transitional divide of adolescence. Adulthood itself now means transition—many transitions between different segments of a life cycle that no longer has a circular shape.

Beyond such general observations concerning the reality of the life cycle and its shape, there are a number of more concrete challenges for the modern idea of adulthood. In the following, I want briefly to take up four of them: the changing role of work, the crisis of marriage and family, the influence of the media, and the situation of religion. Let us first look at the role of work in adulthood.

For example, although it has not been so obvious in the United States, beginning in the 1990s adults in many countries around the world started suffering a deep threat to their status as modern adults because of unemployment. Because of globalization and the international competition that has taken hold of the labor market, many adults experience that paid work has become scarce and often is not attainable for them. Unemployment takes away one of the traditionally most important achievements of proper adulthood, especially for men but also for women—autonomy in the sense of financial independence. It means falling back into a very palpable form of dependence—having to rely on the resources of parents or relatives or on benefits from the state. In addition, unemployment, especially when it is prolonged, often means a severe breakdown of time perspectives and of the time management of the person, and this for everyday life as well as for the structuring of the personal future. Without paid work, there is no more defined schedule for daily life, and without work-related career perspectives, the future threatens to become pointless and empty. This is a critical and possibly devastating experience that many modern adults may go through at the point of retirement, when they leave their work lives behind. Now this experience may come as early as the beginning of adulthood itself—with so-called youth unemployment that really means the denial of access for young people wanting to join the work force.

As mentioned before, unemployment has not been a serious problem in the United States in the last decade, at least not on the surface. Yet American sociologists like Wade Clark Roof caution us not to perceive the situation and outlooks of younger Americans all too brightly. Roof observes:

> Young people face an uncertain economic future. Contrary to the widely held belief that youth is the best time of one's life, young people now constitute one of the most disadvantaged and vulnerable groups in the entire population. As we have moved from an industrial to a post-industrial economy over the past several decades, young people have become disenfranchised. We have told youth that they need education, and they do, but the fact of the matter is that today's youth live in an educationally inflated world. Numerous jobs that once required only a high school education now require a university education, even though the jobs are virtually the same. We educate our children more than we did in the past, and still many youth only see for themselves rather dismal prospects for the future: part-time jobs, poor pay, and competition in a global economy where unpredictable market shifts directly affect opportunities.[9]

Roof is not interested here in what this means for the understanding of adulthood in the United States. Yet it is clear that not only unemployment but also the "dismal prospects" that he reports will have their effects on the identification of being a true adult and of being an active member of the workforce.

The next set of changes to be considered here concern what is often perceived as a far-reaching crisis of marriage and family. In chapter 1, we have already seen how much the forms of family life have changed over the last one hundred years and that, especially over the last thirty to forty years, divorce rates have increased dramatically. In the 1990s, the rate was up to more than 50 percent,[10] and there is no indication that the trend has reversed since. And the United States is not the only place where such tendencies can be observed. Rather, many countries in the Western world show a similar picture for marriage and family, most of all with increasing divorce rates, even if they are still somewhat lower than in the United States.[11]

This does not mean that marriage and family have ceased to play an important role in many people's lives. Yet their meaning is clearly changing. Living as an adult no longer means, at least in many cases, having entered a relationship with a spouse that, ideally, will last for the rest of one's life. Instead, it has come to mean dealing with the changing and complex experience of, sometimes, several marriages and consecutive families, which has been called a patchwork or "postfamilial" life.[12] As pointed out previously (in chapter 2), this situation has far-reaching and often detrimental consequences for the children who are affected by it. In the present context of this chapter, we can come to see that it also affects the modern understanding of adulthood. Again, with the changes of marriage and family, adulthood turns out to have lost one of its main characteristics as a stable time of life. Just as with work and employment, adulthood has become a time of transitions and crises in this respect as well.

Next to work and unemployment and to marriage and family, another important experience affecting the status of adulthood has to do with the still growing influence of the media. According to media researchers like Neil Postman, the very distinction between childhood and adulthood has come into flux through the media. In his book *The Disappearance of Childhood,* Postman points out that the modern image of adulthood has a cultural background that is closely related to the media.[13] According to this view, the understanding of adulthood always changes when new media enter the picture. In support of this hypothesis, Postman first looks at the time when printed media became available on a mass basis (which actually took place during the time of the Reformation in Europe when the printing press was introduced). The dominant role that printed materials soon took in all fields of knowledge and information defined the adult as a person who had access to this kind of information. In this understanding, being adult meant being able to read and write. And through that, Postman says, the reading of printed information came to draw an information borderline between childhood and adulthood, which Postman sees as distinctive for the modern notion of adulthood because it is access to this information that characterizes the adult person.

During the second half of the twentieth century, with the enormously growing impact of media that focus on pictures and images rather than on the written word, this borderline begins to dissolve. Now everything is accessible to everyone, at all ages and at all times. For example, the secrets of adult knowledge concerning sexuality or violence no longer exist. Television brings it all to the home for whoever has two eyes through which the images can enter consciousness. According to Postman's hypothesis, the always present and accessible imagery of television melts down the distinction between adults and children, leaving behind a new hybrid that he describes as the child-adult—a fusion of child and adult who, in front of the tube, may not be distinguished anymore.

Just as with other stages of the life cycle, the changes of adulthood also have implications for *religion*. The consequences that these changes bring about for religion are actually complex and ambivalent. In the remainder of this section, I will focus on two of these consequences because they seem to be of special interest for our understanding of adulthood: a reevaluation of secularization and understanding the public role of religion.

As mentioned before, one of the more hopeful signs of our time regarding the religious situation is the growing insight among many observers that secularization by no means defines the future of religion.[14] The "secular city" has not come—instead the city has become a meeting place of many different religions and of a variety of worldviews. In many countries around the world, the influence of traditional religious institutions like the church has decreased markedly and still seems to be on the decline. Yet at the same time, other forms of individual religion and a new interest in spirituality have increased. There is something like a spiritual hunger that was not expected by the modern prophets of secular society.

Our knowledge of the religion or spirituality of today's adults is limited. The available research certainly does not give us a full picture. Yet there is enough ground for a number of important hypotheses.[15]

- *First,* contemporary adults show a great deal of distance from the traditional church, especially in the sense of the mainline churches in the United States or their equivalents in Europe.[16] Even if a great majority of adults, according to their own statements, believe in God, they do not connect their personal faith with that of the church. "Everyone a special case" is the telling title of a recent study on religion in Switzerland.[17] Even this small country, which was the cradle of Reformed theology and a place deeply influenced by Protestant ethics, now has turned into a most variable landscape of religious plurality and of individualized religion.

- *Second,* as adulthood has become a more flexible stage of life, so have religious orientations during adulthood. Religious affiliation no longer is a stable or permanent characteristic that one needs to hold onto as part of one's adult identity. Instead, many adults are more or less actively pursuing their search for what might be meaningful for their lives. In this process, church membership may be changed or dropped altogether. And there is little to no social pressure not to do so.

- *Third* and most interesting in our present context, issues related to the life cycle seem to be one of the main fields of enduring religious interest. How do I find a meaningful life? Do the various segments of my life cycle form a coherent whole? What will become of me after I die? These are some of the questions that seem to keep the process of the spiritual search in adulthood active.[18]

Taken together, these aspects of religion in adulthood once more confirm the understanding that contemporary religion is highly individualized, pluralized, and privatized, as it has often been described by the sociology of religion. Yet this is not the whole picture. As several observers have pointed out, religion may also take on a new public meaning that should not be overlooked.[19] Again, this perception has to do with the question of secularization.

The critical reevaluation of the idea of secularization also entails a new understanding of the public role that religion may have to play in the future. The neat separation between a secular public and private religion is rapidly losing its plausibility vis-à-vis the actual influence of religion on politics. A vivid example may be found in the environmental movements in many countries that, at least in part, are fired by religious motives, or, to mention a very different example, the conservative Christians in the United States. Clearly, in all such cases, politics and religion are not separate. In a similar vein, we may think of the growing feeling and awareness that we need a strong civil society if democracy is to have a future.[20] The megasystems of state and economy obviously are in no position to furnish the ethical basis or the sense of direction that are needed in personal as well as in social life. In this situation, religion—and Christianity in particular—may be considered as prime resources for giving meaning to life and for nurturing responsibility and care. According to the research of sociologists like Robert Wuthnow, Christianity actually does play an important role in fostering the ethical motives of community orientation and voluntarism in many fields.[21] Yet it is easy to see that not all forms of religion or Christian faith are likely to actually function in this way. Privatized religion that only operates within the individual person and that is focused exclusively on the individual life cycle will hardly be effective as a source for public solidarity.

The three different forms of Christianity that modernity has brought about and that I mentioned in the preceeding section—church, individual religion, and public or civil religion—have not ceased to exist in postmodernity. But in some ways the tensions among them have become stronger. A higher degree of individualization and pluralization has deepened the gap between individual religion and the church, and the religious plurality has made it harder to share enough convictions in order to maintain even a civil religion. At the same time, however, some of the clear-cut divisions also have become more flexible and permeable. I have already mentioned the public influence of religion opening up new connections between religion and the public realm that, from the point of view of modernity, was supposed to be secular. In addition to this, I could also mention the growing awareness within the church that there is a need for building bridges between the church as an institution and the personal and religious life of postmodern individuals.

With this in mind, we move on to the final section of this chapter, which deals with possible responses to the challenges of adulthood in postmodernity.

Practical Theology as Midwife for Postmodern Adulthood?

It is easy to see that, especially with adulthood, the postmodern challenges are by no means only detrimental. They may be detrimental from a modern point of view, but they include many healthy possibilities, and they provide a new openness at exactly those points where the modern life cycle tended to become suffocating. New chances seem to arise for a more humane shape of adult life, and these chances and possibilities also pertain to religion. It is liberating to learn that the extenuating expectation of all things becoming more and more secular may actually not hold true and that the future of religion may look much brighter than the prophets of secularization would have had us believe. Also, religious individualization and pluralization may not lead only to the much-criticized supermarket of religions. Rather, they may also mean that the many voices of people who do not conform to the image of modern adulthood may finally be heard. Actually, this is the reason why some theologians assume that there is a close connection between postmodernity and liberation theology.[22]

Yet the possibilities of the postmodern life cycle and of a more humane shape of adulthood will not be realized automatically. Many of the developments mentioned above refer to ambivalent and open processes, and this is why the work of church and theology is needed. To mention only the most obvious example: A strong civil society that is built on solidarity and mutual care will certainly not come about by itself. There are too many counterforces operating in our culture of competition and violence, and there are also too many cases in which religion has not fostered solidarity and mutual care, but has turned into a source of hostility and conflict. So if a strong civil society is the aim, this requires many conscious and deliberate efforts—efforts of encouraging and directing people and of building up respective values and character traits, in childhood and adolescence, but also in adulthood.

In this process of encouraging and directing people, different images of adulthood will play an important role. Modernity's image of the rational and autonomous individual still is of considerable influence, serving as a model or ideal for the true direction of adult life. If this one-sided and distortive ideal is to lose its hold, different models and ideals are needed. This is why I will focus on *new images of faith* that can work in this direction. Given the insecure passage from modern to postmodern adulthood, such images should clearly support people in their search for more healthy and humane forms of life, which can be found in three directions:

• beyond the ideology of rationalism and progress
• beyond the individualism of isolated autonomy
• beyond the privatism of individualized religion

The first two directions refer to two main tendencies of modern culture, that is, rationalism and individualism. The third direction is focused on the religious aspects connected to them.

A critical view of rationalism, individualism, and religious privatism can count on being shared by many people today, within or without the church. Yet in all three respects, it is easier to say what has to be overcome and left behind than to describe clearly what should come afterward. What is to come after rationalism—relativism or even fundamentalism? What is to come after individualism—a new collectivism or even a tribalism of ethnic and cultural groups as many observers fear? And what is to come after religious privatism—a return to the earlier fusion of church and state?

In the remainder of this chapter, I will take up these three questions by looking for alternative images and guiding models for adulthood. It is clear from the beginning that, in doing so, the dangers that arise in the attempt to leave modern adulthood behind must be given due attention and be carefully avoided. And although I am interested in the contribution of church and theology (at the end of the chapter, I will suggest that practical theology should serve as a midwife for postmodern adulthood), the alternative images for guiding adult life cannot come from church and theology alone. Rather, they will have to come from a cooperation between theology and other fields of knowledge and research. This is why I will draw on philosophical and social scientific models as well.

(1) In my understanding, one of the key images that can guide us in the passage toward responsible postrationalism is the image of *second naïveté* offered by the French-American philosopher Paul Ricoeur.[23] This naïveté refers to a life-cycle perspective by suggesting that childhood is the time of naïve beliefs and of uncritical acceptance of the stories and symbols that are offered to the child. With adolescence and adulthood, this naïveté is broken and is replaced by critical thinking in the sense of the Enlightenment, which considers this kind of thinking the ultimate achievement of human reason. Ricoeur, however, postulates that the development of human understanding should continue beyond the point of a critical destruction of earlier beliefs. It should arrive at a point or stage where it can reconstruct and in some sense reappropriate these beliefs.

This is where the idea of a second naïveté enters the picture. It stands for a return to nonrationalist worldviews and identities, for example, in symbol, narrative, and faith, which are appreciated anew. But while this second naïveté clearly transcends the limits of rationalism, the need for rational argument and for modern science and technology is also not denied. Rather, the achievements of modernity are given a new basis in a more comprehensive framework that allows rationality to play its role—a role that is necessary, yet definitely limited in that it may not define the aims of social or cultural development, nor may it be used as the ultimate norm of the human life cycle. Through this inclusion of rational argument and also through its self-conscious and self-reflexive character, this way of moving beyond rationalism avoids the pitfalls of relativism as well as of fundamentalism. We are not returning to premodernity. Rather, a second naïveté regrounds and reframes modernity, holding on to what deserves to be preserved of modernity while, at the same time, being clear about its limitations.

Ricoeur's philosophical image of a second naïveté is also helpful in restoring religion to its proper place in adulthood, and this is no coincidence. It is clearly in the Christian tradition where we may find the presuppositions on which Ricoeur's image draws. Most notably the German theologian Friedrich Schleiermacher coined the image of a *second childhood* in order to offer adults a post-Enlightenment idea of adult religion.[24] And here, with Schleiermacher, it becomes obvious that the image of a second naïveté and of a second childhood is a modern translation of the New Testament image of becoming "like children" (Mt. 18:3).

The perspective of becoming "like children" can also lead to a different attitude toward the ideology of growth, progress, and perfection. When this perspective is understood in the sense of the doctrine of justification by faith and grace rather than by our own achievements, it allows for a new openness toward the imperfect, incomplete, and even fragmentary character of our lives.[25] In this case, this theological view of the self assumes additional meaning. Earlier (in chapter 3) I pointed out that the appreciation of the fragmentary character of human selfhood can help us in dealing with the postmodern experience of a plural self by making us skeptical about the expectation of a unitary self. In the present context, the same skepticism applies to the expectation of a self that is defined by steady growth, self-perfection, and progressive achievement.

(2) The second direction that must be addressed in the transition to a more humane shape of adulthood concerns the move beyond individualism, which, in the modern view, is a close neighbor to rationality. Rationality is seen as the basis for individual autonomy and vice versa. So it is no less important to consider alternative models beyond individualism than in the case of rationalism.

From my point of view, there are two sources from which helpful images have come to us over the last few decades, from feminist psychology and ethics on the one hand and from the new appraisal of community structures on the other. While I will focus on "community" in the next section, the images from feminist psychology will be my first topic. Two powerful and important images from the work of Carol Gilligan and her colleagues can be mentioned here: *responsibility* and *connectedness*.[26] Both images describe an alternative understanding of maturity and adulthood. By pointing toward mature forms of being responsible for oneself, for others, as well as for nature, and by showing anew how maturity may not be adequately understood in terms of individual autonomy alone, they offer important alternatives to an individualistic understanding of human development.

Rather than identifying maturity with independence, they focus on the essentially relational character of human life and, consequently, the need for mature relationships that include both independence as well as dependence. While this alternative view of human development has been uncovered in the context of feminist psychology and of women's life situations, it also applies to men's lives and to their visions of becoming adults. And for both, men and women, the image of connectedness, which includes responsible relationships toward self and others, can be a powerful guide in overcoming the one-sided modern focus on the individual.

Beyond the psychological account of the need for connectedness described so far, this view has important roots in the biblical tradition. The relational character of human life can actually be called the true center of biblical anthropology, that is, of the understanding of what constitutes the human being according to the Bible.[27] From the beginning, the need for relationships is emphasized, including both the relationship to fellow humans (Gen. 2:18: "It is not good that the man should be alone") as well as the relationship to God. In this sense, the critical view of feminist psychology with its emphasis on connectedness has recovered, without making this explicit, a core Christian understanding upon which church and theology can now draw as a resource for the passage to postmodern adulthood.

Without being able to take up the complex question of how adulthood and the postmodern family should go together, I want at least to point out the possible link between the guiding idea of connectedness and what has been called the model of the "egalitarian family" by the Family, Religion, and Culture Project.[28] This type of family is recommended for the postmodern or postindustrial situation:

> Although we recognize that variations will exist, we argue that the new postindustrial ideal should be the egalitarian family in which husband and wife participate relatively equally in paid work as well as in childcare and other domestic responsibilities.[29]

This ideal can be considered as one concrete example for the potential of a more humane shape of adulthood affording both women and men with new possibilities.

(3) The third image that I want to take up here is the image of *community,* which is of special importance for a new vision of the church and for religion in adulthood. In the 1980s and 1990s, that term played an important role in the discussions about communitarianism as well as in Christian ethics.[30] It is not possible here to deal with the corresponding philosophical and ethical debates. Suffice it to say, at least for the present context, that neither an understanding of the church as a more or less closed community is enough, nor does it make sense to refuse the idea of community altogether in order to work toward a purely universalist ethics like, for example, the well-known discourse ethics of Jürgen Habermas.[31] The universalist view has no real place for special communities because such communities are seen as potentially divisive. At the same time, this negative understanding of community is a decisive weakness of any universalist ethics. In its negativity toward community structures, it tends toward an abstract individualism, and, for church

or religion, it leads to religious privatism because the public sphere is envisioned as purely secular.

Yet to see the church only as a community unto itself, which is not concerned with the wider society and even less with its global environment, also amounts to a reductionist view. The gospel, on which the church must ultimately rest, does not support this kind of self-enclosure. Rather, it is public in the sense that it is addressed to all people and that its views of the human being as well as of society hold important ethical implications that are not limited to the church.[32]

The perspective for a future beyond religious individualism and privatism requires a vision for church and religion that is limited neither to abstract universalism nor to a self-enclosed community. A community that thinks only of itself and that cares only for its members clearly contradicts the self-understanding of the Christian faith, which extends love and care even to the enemy. In this sense, I want to call the church a *public community*. It is a community based on a shared faith. But it is also a community that addresses the public and that works toward the common good. From a different perspective, it has been called a "public church," a designation that also points out the public nature of the church.[33]

The modern notion of adulthood is premised on the clear division between church, private religion, and public responsibility. At the beginning of this new century, it has become obvious that this division no longer fits the needs of personal and social life. Rather, it creates many problems: for the future of democracy and civil society, which is in need of moral and religious support; for the individual person whose life becomes empty and shallow if all questions of meaning and truth are confined to the inner world of feelings; and also for the church, which cannot fulfill its mission if it is separated from the personal as well as from the public domain.

To the degree that the contemporary experiences of postmodern life allow for overcoming the division between church, individual, and public religion, they may turn out to be beneficial. This statement does not stand for an undue optimism. Rather, it points toward the task of a practical theology that positions itself at the point of transition between modernity and postmodernity and that has to offer guiding images for the future—images of community and responsibility, of connectedness, and of a second naïveté, not only for individual religion or for a secular public but for the sake of a new type of public religious presence.

CHAPTER 6

Between Adulthood and Old Age

The Question of a "Third Age"

Although my main emphasis in this study is on those stages that sometimes are summarized metaphorically as the first two thirds of the life cycle, that is, the span from childhood to adulthood, we would be clearly mistaken to assume that changes are only happening during those times in life. It is true that the changes affecting childhood and adolescence have received much more attention in the past than those in adulthood or old age. Even a developmental psychology of adulthood is a fairly recent phenomenon, entering the picture only forty to fifty years ago.[1] Before then, most psychologists took for granted that development comes to its end with the transition from adolescence to adulthood as the time of maturity. Yet as I have tried to show in the preceding chapter in respect to images of faith and adulthood, the adult stage of the life cycle can include many major developmental (sub)stages, and this has become generally accepted in the psychology of religion as well.[2] But only recently has it become more common to also include a special focus on religion in old age.

With this background in mind, it is easy to understand why a chapter on old age was not part of my original plan for this book. My earlier work on childhood, adolescence, and adulthood had led me to believe that the most important changes to be addressed in this study would certainly be found in the early stages of the life cycle.[3] Those who attended my lectures on such topics, however, soon made me aware of the need to carry my analysis of the changing shape of the life cycle even further by also including its later stages. And indeed, they were right. Whoever is interested in the postmodern life cycle and in its challenges for church and theology cannot close their eyes to old age.

According to the temporal logic of the modern life cycle, the stage of adulthood is followed by "old age," the last stage of the life cycle. It is important to note from the beginning that this sequence is not just a result of human nature in a biological sense. Rather, the understanding of old age as a life-cycle stage is clearly modeled on the identification of adulthood with (paid) work. In this view, a new phase of life begins with retirement, and this phase is characterized by its position at the end of life as the terminal stage. It is exactly at this point that more recent developments and contemporary interpretations of the life cycle have taken issue with the traditional or modern view. According to Peter Laslett, whose work has exerted considerable international influence in this field of discussion, we have to let go of our traditional assumptions concerning the sequence of adulthood and old age in order to consider the possibility of another age or stage, which comes into the picture *after* modern adulthood but clearly *before* the last stage of life.[4] Laslett calls this additional age the "Third Age," distinguishing it from the Second Age (modern adulthood) and from the Fourth Age (old age or senility, the terminal stage of life). It is this distinction to which I am referring in the title of this chapter. Laslett's critique of the traditional model of the life cycle and its application to old age can alert us to the need to consider another new stage within the life cycle, just as we had to consider the emergence of postadolescence as a new stage at an earlier point of this study.

The question of late adulthood or old age also raises important questions concerning the religious implications of the changes to be observed in respect to adulthood and old age. For a long time, church and theology did not give any special attention to this age group, which seemed to be quite content with what the church was offering them. Recently, however, observers in different countries have pointed out that such offerings might, in fact, be based on views of old age that are no longer accurate and that cannot do justice to the real needs and potentials of the people concerned.[5] Given that many Western societies clearly have turned into aging societies in that the percentage of older adults is becoming a larger and larger segment of the population, these are indeed alarming signs for church and theology.

Traditional Expectations: Beyond the Obligations of Adulthood— The Wisdom of Disengagement

It is probably fair to say that modernity has produced especially contradictory expectations concerning late adulthood and old age. On the one hand, it has created the idea of a time in life that promises to be something like a reward for having worked hard most of one's life. On the other hand, the identification of the adult person with the autonomous individual described in chapter 5 above has made it especially difficult to appreciate the status of no longer pursuing paid work and to enjoy this reward. What can a life be in this view, if this life is no longer productive and progressive in terms of professional achievement? Can there be any meaning and value in it if it no longer matches the standards of independence and autonomy? The important improvements in health care that have been characteristic of modernity have strengthened both tendencies, and they have further emphasized the tensions and contradictions between them. Good health is needed in order to enjoy the benefits of a nonworking life in late adulthood. This clearly is a positive effect of modern medicine. Yet the higher and higher life expectancy has also led to the widespread concern about if and how a society will be able to sustain itself if more and more of its members no longer participate in the production of goods and in making services available.[6] Modern old age clearly has economic implications.

It is a well-known fact that the twentieth century has brought about a new pattern for late adulthood and old age.[7] Through the introduction of pension funds or other retirement benefits, the status of having retired from work has become generalized and has become available for all or most members of this age group in Western countries. To be sure, there have always been individuals who could afford this enjoyable kind of retirement, even long before modernity. But the majority of the population had no chance to ever acquire and accumulate the considerable resources that are needed for having financial security in old age. The new availability of financial resources for mass retirement has certainly solved or at least mitigated a number of serious problems that older members of society had to face at earlier times, most of all the fate of old age poverty or lack of health care. Yet it has also created a most difficult transition at the end of one's working career. After having striven for, and having achieved, a position within working life, and after having defined oneself through this position, many people find it extremely difficult to accept and to appreciate a new and different status that is based exactly on *not* having this kind of position anymore. The many discussions about the existential crises accompanying the transition into retirement testify to this. Other indicators are the various offers of psychological counseling and support for those who prepare for, or actually are going through, this transition at the end of a professional career.

Erik Erikson's model of the life cycle again proves to be highly interesting in this context. Erikson describes the central crisis of maturity or old age by pointing out the tension between "integrity" and "despair."[8] As the positive pole in this tension, "integrity" takes over from "generativity," the positive pole in Erikson's view of adulthood. The question of integrity implies a far-reaching change of perspectives. While generativity necessarily implies looking ahead because whatever is to be "generated" or achieved can only lie in the future, integrity means looking back at one's past and present. Therefore, it means the "acceptance of one's one and only life cycle as something that had to be."[9] The most serious and truly existential challenge of looking at one's life in such a retrospective manner arises from the fact that we cannot change the past. A life that has been lived must now either be appreciated as something meaningful ("something that *had* to be") or be rejected in "despair" and disgust because of the chances and possibilities that one did not use when there was still time to do so. As we will see below, the question of integrity, of coming to terms with one's life retrospectively, has important religious implications. But before considering the religious dimensions of old age, we first have to look into a number of additional aspects of old age in modernity.

Sometimes, it is assumed that old people used to be well respected in earlier times of history. This assumption refers especially to the so-called wisdom of old age that is based on the accrued experience of a lifetime. In contrast to this, modernity is supposed to have devalued the status of old people as well as the importance of knowledge accumulated in the past. With its focus on future progress, modernity has no place for what is related to the past. Recently, however, historians have contested this view.[10] According to them, old people have always been subject to negative attitudes within the younger generation, at least to some degree, and it seems that stereotypes directed against old people were no less abundant in the Middle Ages than they are in modernity. Yet even if we must be cautious not to idealize the attitudes toward old age in premodern times, there can be no doubt that so-called ageism is a serious problem encountered in the twentieth (and twenty-first) century.

The term *ageism* refers to hostile and denigrating views of old people.[11] As a prejudice, it associates old age with dependence and inability, with a general loss of value for people who no longer are able to work. Ageism is a kind of stereotyping in that it generalizes certain aspects of old age, thus turning them into an overall negative image that leaves no place for other, possibly more positive, aspects.

As mentioned before, such problematic views must be seen in light of the general changes of the age structure of society. Many Western societies have turned into aging societies, that is, they include higher and higher percentages of older people.[12] Social scientists consider the "graying of America" as inevitable, and they expect severe consequences for the economy.[13] When the number of old people living in a society is growing fast, this can intimidate the younger members of society. Are they to carry the burden of taking care of and feeding an ever-larger number of people who are no longer able or willing to work? Population statistics show that life expectancies in the Western world have increased considerably. In fact, it seems that the last hundred years have been the time for this to happen, which explains why the realization of this change has been something like a shock. We are not talking about a slow process of change over many centuries but about a rapidly changing situation. In England, for example, where these patterns have been researched intensively, a child born in the year 1900 could statistically expect a lifetime of a little more than forty years. By the end of the century, the figure was up to somewhere between seventy and eighty years. And during the same period of time the percentage of the over sixty-year-olds in England doubled from a little more than 10 percent to about 20 percent.[14] Such figures indicate how much the situation has changed, and that the meaning of age has become rather flexible.

What about traditional (modern) expectations concerning *religion* in old age? As mentioned above, Erikson's model makes religious questions a central dimension of the last stage of the life cycle. In a certain sense, the adolescent identity crisis repeats itself at this point, including its religious aspects but now with a different perspective. The adolescent identity crisis is premised on the young person's looking ahead and looking out for meaningful ends to be achieved in his or her future life. According to Erikson, religion contributes to the successful resolution of this crisis by offering a meaningful way of viewing the world and of interpreting history, so that adolescents can find their place in it. Contrary to this, old persons are looking back to the lives that they have led and that they cannot change anymore, at least not in many ways or only to a limited degree. Dissatisfaction or "despair" arises when this life cannot be accepted. But how can this devastating experience be avoided? Again, Erikson speaks of a religious need at this stage that is similar to the need in adolescence.

He calls it "some world order and spiritual sense."[15] In a central passage, Erikson writes about the religious "wisdom" needed at this stage:

> Strength here takes the form of that detached yet active concern with life bounded by death, which we call *wisdom*...Not that each man evolves wisdom for himself. For most, a living *tradition* provides the essence of it. But the end of the cycle also evokes "ultimate concerns" for what chance man may have to transcend the limitations of his identity and his often tragic or bitterly tragicomic engagement in his one and only life cycle within the sequence of generations. Yet great philosophical and religious systems dealing with ultimate individuation seem to have remained responsibly related to the cultures and civilizations of their times. Seeking transcendence by renunciation, they yet remain ethically concerned with the "maintenance of the world."[16]

And in the same context, Erikson also addresses the parallels between religion in adolescence and religion in old age, referring to "a new edition" of the adolescent crisis of identity:

> To whatever abyss ultimate concerns may lead individual men, man as a psychosocial creature will face, toward the end of his life, a new edition of an identity crisis which we may state in the words "I am what survives of me."[17]

Although Erikson does not offer a detailed description of how despair and disgust can be outweighed by wisdom sponsored by a religious or spiritual tradition, it is easy to see that the final crisis of the life cycle is a deeply religious crisis. Religious understandings of death and afterlife will be of great help to a person who is wondering about the meaning of his or her life as it is now approaching the end.

Research data on church membership and on participation in Sunday worship services clearly support the expectations based on this theoretical point of view. Interest in religion becomes stronger in late adulthood and old age. Correspondingly, congregations often comprise a considerable number of older adults and only few active members between the age of twenty and fifty or sixty.[18]

Although there seems to be a good match between the expectation that religion has an important role to play in late adulthood or old age and the actual participation of older people in the church, there also are critical questions concerning the ambivalences created by this situation. As mentioned in chapter 5, there is the concern that associating religion with adolescence on the one hand, and with old age on the other excludes the meaning of religion in most of adulthood. This way of viewing religion as a matter only for children and for old people clearly contradicts the self-understanding of the Christian faith as comprising all of life and as giving shape and orientation to all ages, including adulthood. In addition to this, there is at least some evidence (considered in chapter 4) that the traditional patterns of the life cycle—adolescents moving away from the church in order to come back to it later in life—cannot necessarily be taken for granted anymore, and that in the future, given today's lack of religious involvement in earlier stages, there may not be such a return to the church in late adulthood or old age.

Finally, the programs offered by the church have been criticized for not taking old people seriously enough.[19] In this view, such programs fit all too well with the understandings maintained by a dated gerontology. Generally speaking, many programs offered for older adults by the church follow the logic of *taking care* of them. Either they are designed to support people as they become weaker and more dependent, or, on the contrary, they are trying to activate old people in order to keep them as young and healthy as possible. The first option corresponds to the theory of *disengagement,* which is focused on aspects like weakness, fragility, dependence, and disability in old age. The second option follows from the theory of *activation,* which has its focus on the possibility of counteracting senility by keeping old people active. Many researchers consider both theories as outdated.[20] In different ways, both the theory of disengagement and the theory of activation are criticized for not doing justice to the complex realities of life in old age. And even more important, neither approach takes old people seriously as responsible subjects who are not looking for treatments and who do not want to be taken care of. As we will see in the next section, this critical evaluation is strongly supported by the views connected to postmodernity and to the changes to be observed with older adulthood and old age today.

Postmodern Challenges: Redesigning the Life Cycle?

In the beginning of this chapter, I mentioned the observation that what used to be the straightforward sequence of adulthood and old age has changed to such a degree that it may make sense to speak of a new phase or additional stage in the life cycle. Let us consider some of these changes that have made the traditional sequence more and more questionable.

A first observation concerns the high level of activity maintained by many of those who, according to their age, fall under the category of old age. Rather than following the pattern of being content with looking back at one's life, they develop new ideas and start new projects. Travel in old age is one example; volunteer work in the congregation or community is another. The growing number of older adults returning to the university or participating in serious educational programs has rightly received a lot of attention. In this case, learning and being trained, which in the logic of modernity used to be associated almost exclusively with the future-oriented investments of adolescents or young adults, are becoming attractive to older adults as well.

Another important experience is related to the situation of women, especially to women whose primary occupation is homemaking and childcare rather than paid employment. For them, the period between the time when the last child leaves the home and the time when they reach the age of sixty-five or seventy has become longer and longer.[21] Several factors have contributed to this change, which can be observed over the last fifty to one hundred years. The average number of children per family has decreased, so that the duration of active parenthood has become shorter, often ending in the forties when the last child leaves the home. The idea that women at this age move from generativity to integrity, from active life to looking back at activities in their past, is not very plausible. In fact, the situation of not having to take care of the children anymore but also of not having a job in the sense of paid labor is often experienced as depressing. It is experienced as imposed not by any natural course of life but rather by a society that, due to gender specific ageism, has no space for the interests and needs of the women in this age group.

Experiences and observations of this kind have led to the idea that we have to rethink our traditional assumptions about late adulthood and old age. The expectation that working life is followed by inactive retirement and by being taken care of has turned out to be a stereotype or even an ideology. As mentioned in the beginning of this chapter, one of the most productive responses to this situation has come from the British historian and social researcher Peter Laslett. In his book, aptly called *A Fresh Map of Life,* he traces the "emergence of a Third Age." He wants systematically to distinguish and separate four different ages:

> First comes an era of dependence, socialization, immaturity and education; second an era of independence, maturity and responsibility, of earning and of saving; third an era of personal fulfillment; and fourth an era of final dependence, decrepitude and death.[22]

The main reason for introducing this distinction is the need to reconsider the meaning of old age under the present circumstances of having a larger and larger segment of retired people in society. The traditional characteristics of dependence and weakness are no longer sufficient for doing justice to the different realities of life at this age. And most of all, such negative images fail to give the time of the Third Age a purpose of its own. This is why Laslett is eager to point out the new opportunities and possibilities that come after the many obligations of the Second Age, the obligations of paid work, have ended. And this is also the reason for his suggestion to consider the Third Age as a time with high potential for personal fulfillment, which becomes possible when the constraints of a career lose their hold on a person's life.

Laslett is well aware of the many questions that his idea of a Third Age and of personal fulfillment inevitably encounters, especially in relationship to the employment of older people after the age of retirement, which he discusses, but also in terms of the high expectations for potential fulfillment. In the present context, however, I am less interested in a discussion of Laslett's personal views, which we can leave to the specialists in the social scientific research on old age. What is of central importance for my own purposes is what Laslett's approach indicates. In my understanding, his idea of a Third Age is related to far-reaching changes of the modern (traditional) understanding of old age as the time after retirement from work and, at the same time, as the last stage of life. The traditional view does not do justice to the experiences of many people whose lives do not fit this simple pattern anymore. These experiences are the basis for assuming a new and additional stage of the life cycle, which is located between what used to be called adulthood and old age.

So it is no surprise that the traditional (modern) views of older adulthood or old age have come under criticism, whether through the work of historians and philosophers such as Laslett or through empirical research on old age today. On the basis of recent empirical studies, social scientists have argued that generalizations about old age are more and more likely to miss the realities of life in old age.[23] According to their observations, individualization has strongly affected this stage of the life cycle, no less than is the case with the earlier ones. Becoming older, it is said, is most of all an individual process that, for its concrete characteristics, very much depends on individual circumstances, which cannot be generalized. Consequently, these researchers reject large-scale theories of old age and are trying to replace them with sensitive descriptions that are open for individual life situations and for personal evaluations by the people themselves. As we will see in the next section below, this raises interesting questions for practical theology and the church. But before considering these questions, we need to again turn to religion in old age.

Religion in late adulthood and old age has not received much attention in research at all. Until recently, psychologists of religion tended to focus almost exclusively on childhood and adolescence, which were seen as the decisive periods of religious development. In the meantime, the picture has changed but only to a certain degree. While psychologists and gerontologists have made available a considerable body of research on religion in old age, the focus of this research is rather narrow and is often defined by a medical context.[24] Most of the research carried out in the field of gerontology is related to questions of physical health and emotional strength, which points to the fact that such studies are more focused on what Laslett calls the Fourth Age of senility than on the Third Age, which, as a time of new possibilities, comes before senility. The religious dimensions of wisdom to which Erikson refers,[25] for example, or the spiritual development of older adults, are rarely studied on their own behalf.

A good and interesting example of this kind of research is Harold G. Koenig's *Aging and God: Spiritual Pathways to Mental Health in Midlife and Later Years,* which comes out of the Program on Religion, Aging, and Health at Duke University.[26] The focus of Koenig's study is on psychological problems like depression and anxiety. The researchers on whose work Koenig is drawing are interested in people's use of religion in coping with such problems. Beyond this concern, Koenig also offers a helpful list of "spiritual needs," which he sees closely connected to old age.[27] The fourteen spiritual needs comprised by this list include, for example, the "need for meaning, purpose, and hope" or the "need to love and serve others," which points to what Laslett and others have identified as the potentials of a Third Age. Yet it is also characteristic of Koenig's approach that his list ends with the "need for preparation for death and dying." This indicates that it is again the terminal stage or the end of life that really is in view here and that shapes this consideration of spiritual needs.

If it is true, however, that changes in society have created the potential for something like the Third Age described by Laslett, a set of entirely different questions arises, questions that have not been addressed in the traditional approaches to religion in old age because they are not related to the end of life. We will consider at least some of them in the following section.

Taking Up the Challenge: Designing Models of Ministry and Education for the Third Age

Let us assume that a Third Age really exists and that at least some people have come to realize the possibilities of this stage for themselves. How will they view the programs offered to them by the church? It is easy to see that persons in their Third Age will not feel attracted by programs that advertise support for "the elderly" and care for the "frail." They do not want to be taken care of. And they also do not feel that their needs or interests are addressed when death and dying are the only topics on which they are supposed to meditate. Rather, just like younger adults, they are looking for opportunities to do something meaningful with the new freedom that they have achieved after their earlier obligations to work or family have ended. And often they are willing to explore possibilities that they were forced to leave aside because of the many constraints on time connected to a working life or to the preparation for this kind of life and career.

Sales and marketing specialists have long realized the potential of this growing group of customers. One has only to look through the advertisement sections of popular magazines in order to recognize how advertisers view their target groups in late adulthood and early old age. Their central topics have little to do with being weak, dependent, or senile. Rather, they refer to unfulfilled longings, long-harbored wishes, and new potentials to be developed. Often they seem to envision–and to promise–a life that finally can be enjoyed.

Of course, I am not arguing here for the church to make popular advertising its guiding model. The task of the church is not to become another source of pleasure that feeds on consumerism. And I am also not in favor of church-sponsored programs to join the widespread repression of the darker sides of life. This avoidance, as can be seen from the example of death and dying, can only result in the contradictory attitude of not talking about it but being even more fascinated or frightened by it and therefore taking refuge, from time to time, in the consumption of popular self-help books on dealing with death and dying.

The life promised to older people by target-group advertising is certainly ambivalent. But once we leave aside the absurdities of contemporary consumerism, there also is something to be learned by church and theology from how others view and address people in late adulthood and early old age. It seems to me that their views clearly confirm Laslett's conviction that we have to appreciate the emerging Third Age by creating space for it and by offering new opportunities to those at this stage in life.

But what does this mean for the church? Three interrelated tasks are of special importance: to develop a theological understanding of the new stage of a Third Age; to design strategies for supporting the potential of this stage; to offer opportunities for people at this age that do justice to this potential.

(1) I am well aware that the Third Age is still an open question and not a reality. But if we keep this in mind, it still makes sense to think ahead theologically and to develop a theological understanding of this new stage of the life cycle. As we have seen above, the meaning of old age is far from being a natural given. It is subject to social conventions, and it is always dependent on what possibilities are available for older people. In this sense, church and theology are actively involved in defining and redefining old age. Their views and their designs for older people are part of the social expectations that give shape to this stage of the life cycle.

It is important to realize that older people themselves are redefining their status. Therefore, it is no coincidence that there seems to be an emerging new view of ministry with older people.[28] More and more, the idea of taking care of them proves insufficient. More and more frequently, there are references to a "new type" of older persons who want to be actively involved in planning and creating programs and in forming groups for special purposes. But what does this mean in terms of a theological understanding of life at this stage?

Traditionally, since well before the onset of modernity, death, dying, and the afterlife have been of special concern for theology and the church. Ancient concepts such as *ars moriendi*, the art of dying, or *meditatio mortis*, the meditation of death and human finitude, testify to this concern. Another issue for theology and the church that clearly goes back to biblical times is respect for old people who no longer are able to work ("Honor your father and your mother," Ex. 20:12) or who are in need of special protection, for example, widows (1 Tim. 5). These issues remain important, and I will come back to them in the final section of this chapter. Yet it is also easy to see that theology and the church have to go beyond their traditional focus on the terminal stage of life if they are to do justice to the emerging life-cycle stage before senility.

The changing shape of late adulthood and old age challenges theology and the church to acknowledge and to appreciate that a longer life expectancy demands a meaningful period of life *after* retirement and *before* senility.[29] This period does not fit the traditional patterns to which theology and the church had to refer in earlier times. This is why the Christian tradition does not contain direct references to this new stage of life. But it is nevertheless possible to appreciate this stage as a gift from God, just as all of life must be seen as God's gift. And this view includes the prospect that life in the Third Age should be treated–and enjoyed–respectfully and responsibly as a new opportunity.

In terms of practical church work, this new understanding of late adulthood, which reckons with the possibility of a Third Age, should encourage us to face up to new issues and tasks that have little to do with the traditional topics of church work in old age but that are closely connected to the potentials of a new stage of the life cycle.

(2) Supporting people in their attempts to realize the potential of a Third Age is of crucial importance because of the ambivalence that we encounter at this point. What I said in chapter 5 about the tensions and contradictions of modern adulthood also applies to late adulthood and old age. The danger of excluding certain adults from the status of full adulthood because they no longer are autonomous ("earning") individuals is especially pertinent in the case of postretirement. Theology and the church must therefore develop strategies that, at the same time, are critical in respect to such tendencies and are supportive of the people by giving space to their needs.

Creating space for the Third Age so that more people can realize the potential of an adult life after the obligations of work and family have ended really means to act as a *midwife* for these emerging possibilities. It means making sure that advertising and consumerism are not allowed to be the only defining forces in this field. To put it differently: The new status offered to older people in advertisements and in the popular literature on old age is highly ambivalent. This status rightly refers to the potential and possibilities of old age, which have been denied by modern society because of modernity's focus on work, autonomy, and progress. But if this new status, which is being created now, does not leave space for weakness and dependence anymore, it will be no less oppressive than the situation before it. So practical theology as a midwife to postmodern old age–the Third Age–must do the following: first, help this age to come about by making space for it; second, help people to reflect critically on modern ideologies that equate adulthood with independence, but also reflect on the promises of commercial target-group advertising that has been so quick in discovering the growing number of older customers; and third, make available alternatives to old-age consumerism.

In light of the background of this threefold task or strategy, we are now in a position to address the question of which opportunities a church or congregation should offer to the people of this age group.

(3) One idea that has sometimes also become a reality in some congregations is volunteer work carried out by older people. This is an important development in that older people are reclaiming their status as subjects, rather than being only the objects, of church activities. But given the demands of a Third Age, not just any type of voluntary work within the church will do. If older adults should be enabled to make use of their new and unrealized potential, it is not enough to offer them substitute duties that otherwise would have to be carried out by paid personnel. And it is also not enough to expect the volunteers of the Third Age to be waiting for a pastor to tell them what to do and how to do it. If the church wants to help people in making use of their new possibilities, the church must be willing to change. There clearly is a need for a place where the members of this age group can come together without needing a special occasion and without consumerism as the basis for shared activities. Possibly some kind of tearoom or coffeehouse located in the church could serve this purpose, or there could be a special community center that is designed for this purpose. Given the lack of successful models, there is much leeway for congregations to experiment with new ideas and possibilities. But since this age group is still growing and as it is becoming more important in society, congregations would be well advised to make a conscious decision about how they want to handle this group.

There is another reason why meaningful volunteer work is important in this context. If this kind of work is connected to the idea of a public church, as mentioned in chapter 5, it takes on additional meaning in several important ways. The public church is a community that is not only focused on itself but has a lasting interest in society as a whole. It is connected to the Christian commitment to the whole community as well as to future generations. This is why it can create a meaningful horizon for combining both the search for personal fulfillment by taking on new tasks and by discovering new things on the one hand, and the responsibility of a Christian life on the other.

What opportunities that do justice to the potential of older people can be offered? It is obvious that this is a field for future experimentation, and that we cannot yet draw on many successful examples. It will, however, probably be helpful to consider at least a number of directions to be pursued in this context.

- *Study groups* of all kinds can offer opportunities for exploring new interests and meeting new people. Topics should come not only from theology or a church context but should also include questions of personal development, music and theater, and so forth. And such groups should not always be organized by a pastor or adult educator but should be, wherever possible, under the leadership of the people concerned themselves.

- *Travel programs* are often organized by commercial enterprises catering to those whose financial assets make them interesting customers. This is actually one of the reasons why the church should think of organizing noncommercial programs that are more affordable and, consequently, less exclusive. Another reason has to do with how such programs are planned. Although some of the commercial programs are quite acceptable educationally, many of them do not offer anything beyond the promise of pleasure and entertainment. In contrast, travel programs that are in line with theological and educational expectations could include, for example, a serious encounter with different cultures or religions, with different churches, or with groups of similar age in different countries. And maybe such encounters could even become part of an international movement for peace and mutual understanding, like the exchange programs offered for youth.

- *Community services* also have a tradition within congregations. Soup kitchens or food pantries, for example, play an important role in many communities. Such activities should definitely be valued in the present context as well, especially in terms of their meaning for a public church. The guiding model of a public church can also become an impulse for pursuing the issue of community services even further—for example, by extending it to the challenges of public life in a community. What can be done, for example, in order to facilitate the acceptance of minorities in the community? How can we support mutual understanding and acceptance between different religious groups beyond Christianity?

- *Intergenerational learning* and *mentorships* are less well-known possibilities within congregations. The concept of intergenerational learning suggests that different generations will profit equally from working together and from learning together in fields of recent interest, such as ecological issues that often are important to young people, or peace issues in relation to globalization. Research on adult development has stressed the importance of older adults acting as mentors for younger ones.[30] While such mentorships have traditionally had their place within the context of work, it would certainly be possible to extend them into different contexts like the congregation. Intergenerational programs could be of help in creating the points of contact that are needed in order to get mentoring relationships started.

• *Church development* is often seen as a task only for pastors. Yet it is easy to see that the inclusion of other members of the congregation can be a powerful way for extending the scope of this development. In the present context, it must be emphasized, however, that the point is not to gain additional help in the pastorate but to allow people to realize their potential. And this includes, in the first place, allowing them to articulate their own ideas about how they want the church to develop. And it also means to let them work not *under* the supervision of the pastors, but as their partners and coworkers.

Much more could be said about these exemplary perspectives, which certainly are demanding and challenging for many congregations. But in the end, it is less important which perspective will be taken up in a given congregation than that the overall task of doing justice to the needs and potentials of a new age group is realized.

The Last Step: Life unto Death—Between Modern Exclusion and New Appropriation

Even the heralds of a Third Age and its possibilities must be aware of the danger of denying the need for thinking about death and dying as part of the human condition. It would be detrimental to repress this aspect of our existence. Consequently, there would be good reasons to include a whole chapter on this topic, which could again give us occasion to address the changing shape of the human life cycle, for example, in relationship to society's ways of including and excluding death in its daily routines. Yet in order to keep this study at a reasonable length, I will limit myself to a brief section on what I metaphorically call the last step. This section serves two limited but important purposes.

The first purpose is to make sure that my focus on the Third Age in this chapter is not misunderstood in such a way that theology and the church should give up their concern with death and dying. The concepts of *ars moriendi* and of *meditatio mortis*, the art of dying and the meditation of death, viewed in the light of the Christian hope for resurrection, must remain of central importance in their work.

The second purpose has to do with modernity's view of death and dying. In this respect, I want to point out that there is a need for overcoming this view and that postmodern alternatives to this view should indeed be pursued if they open up new possibilities.

Many sociologists and researchers in this field have shown that modernity has no real place for the experience of finitude and death.[31] They argue that modern societies have tended to exclude death from visibility by confining it to places like special hospitals and to isolated wards even within such hospitals. Modernity's optimism and belief in progress are deeply challenged by the finitude and the ultimate limitations of human life on earth. This is why death and dying are often repressed and turned into a taboo.

Another issue, which recently has received a fair amount of attention, is the influence of modern medical technology. Often, this technology keeps people medically alive long after they have ceased to be in contact with other people and long after most of their vital functions have ended. Many people are wondering if this can really be for the good of the patients or for their survivors.

The flip side of the repression of death and dying is the remarkable fascination with death and dying that modernity has also produced at certain times. One of the most impressive examples is the public reaction to the interviews published by Elisabeth Kübler-Ross in her bestselling book *On Death and Dying*.[32] Lectures based on this book have turned the experiences of her interviewees into an international media event of considerable popularity. Repression and dramatization by the media can obviously go hand in hand, but they do not lead to healthier attitudes vis-à-vis human finitude.

It is an open question as to whether or not postmodernity has afforded us with more appropriate possibilities in this respect. Our contemporary situation includes some hopeful signs, such as the hospice movement with its commitment to allowing people a more humane experience of approaching death. Yet the overall situation appears generally unchanged. The challenge of overcoming modernity's ambivalence toward death and dying still lies ahead of us.

CHAPTER 7

Theological Demands on Postmodern Life

Toward a Theology of the Life Cycle

This last chapter serves several purposes. First, I want to come back to some of the questions and problems that we encountered in the beginning of the book. The issue of the postmodern life cycle, which I have traced through childhood, adolescence, postadolescence, adulthood, and old age, and the challenges that the changing shape of the life cycle entails for church and theology are the main topics of this chapter. In this sense, my study is meant to be a contribution to Christian praxis as it encounters the needs and challenges of contemporary life and culture.

Second, the encounter with the postmodern life cycle also implies far-reaching theoretical questions that concern the nature of practical theology in its relationship to postmodernity. Does this relationship allow for practical theology to stay the same? Or is there a need for a new practical theology—a new paradigm as some people like to call it, a postmodern paradigm of practical theology?

Third, this chapter will address the question of theological demands on postmodern life, as I called it in the first chapter of this book. So far, my main emphasis has been on the demands posed by postmodernity. Consequently, my focus was on adaptations to be made by church and theology in order to keep pace with postmodernity. But as we have seen in several respects throughout this study, this is not the whole story. We also have to be explicit in the opposite direction by making theology our starting point and by asking about theological demands on postmodern life. What are the demands or criteria that can help theology move toward a critical and constructive encounter with postmodernity? What kind of practical theology do we need for this purpose?

It may be helpful to start by reviewing some of the questions concerning this kind of theology and by summing up some of the pertinent arguments contained in the chapters of this book.

Open Questions

It seems fair to say that, on the whole, practical theology has not fully dealt with the issue of postmodernity.[1] In part, especially in Western Europe, this is due to the second thoughts that have been raised about the idea of postmodernity. Does postmodernity really exist? Will the concept of postmodernity help us in diagnosing contemporary culture or is it actually a misleading and, at best, shaky category? While the idea of postmodernity is considered vague or even depressive and nostalgic, concepts of modernity and modernization still exert a continuing influence on the European side of the Atlantic. In the United States, however, the concept of postmodernity seems much more accepted, and a considerable number of theological studies have taken it up, most notably in exegesis and in systematic theology.[2] Yet even in the North American discussion, at least to my knowledge, no major study on practical theology and postmodernity has been published yet.

The hesitancy to be observed with practical theology vis-à-vis postmodernity may also be due to the empirical aspects connected to this concept. In this respect, the situation appears quite unclear. Philosophical analyses such as, for example, the accounts offered by David Harvey or Wolfgang Welsch have been widely accepted as standard views on postmodernity.[3] But are these views also valid empirically with respect to contemporary forms of everyday life? May we presuppose, for example, that the stages of the life cycle have actually changed according to the expectations formulated in philosophy? In general, practical theologians tend to be hesitant to base their understandings and their models of praxis on theoretical and philosophical concepts that have not been established on empirical grounds. And given the fact that some social scientists still consider it unlikely that a postmodern self has actually replaced the modern self, there are good reasons for practical theology to take a more guarded position on the issue of postmodernity.[4] In any case, a more empirical and inductive approach is needed if practical theology is to address the demands of postmodern life.

Yet at the same time, the issue of postmodernity holds a special challenge to practical theology that, if taken seriously, actually makes postmodernity a most pressing issue for practical theology. If it is true, as it is often stated in textbooks, that practical theology as an academic discipline is a child of modernity, then one must wonder if the advent of postmodernity implies that there is no more need for this kind of endeavor. Does the advent of postmodernity, if it exists, mark the end of practical theology? Or, if not, does it call for a new paradigm for practical theology? And if so, how can this child of modernity come of age in postmodern times?

In the approach that I have used in the present study as well as in earlier work on which this study is based, I attempt to combine both questions mentioned above by asking about the changes to be observed empirically with the contemporary life cycle on the one hand, and by asking what these changes imply for practical theology on the other.[5] My choice of the life cycle as the main aspect of postmodernity to be studied is due to the special interest that this aspect holds for practical theology. This special interest is connected to the practical work in church and society that is to be informed and guided by practical theology. At the same time, this interest refers to the relationship between practical theology and postmodernity on a theoretical level. To make the life cycle a central topic of practical theology or to develop a practical theology along the stages of the life cycle can be considered a typically modern approach. This can be seen from the widespread attention that this kind of practical theology has received over the last thirty or forty years, especially in the field of pastoral counseling, where textbooks often take this approach.[6] The view implied in this kind of practical theology is based on the modern understanding of individual life as a presupposition for theology. More specifically, it is the life of the autonomous individual that, according to this view, determines the horizon that modern practical theology must accept as its starting point.[7] Consequently, considering the relationship between the changes of the life cycle and practical theology may help us in gaining a better understanding of the current situation of practical theology.

My focus on the changes of the life cycle in the present study is also motivated by the search for an inductive approach to the question of postmodernity. As mentioned in chapter 1, this inductive approach cannot be naïve in that it is in fact impossible to approach phenomena such as postmodernity in an exclusively empirical manner. Throughout this study, we had to make use of concepts and categories from the philosophical discussion in order to decipher contemporary experiences. Yet by asking about postmodern life and about the postmodern life cycle rather than limiting ourselves to a philosophical analysis, we could at least get closer to the actual experiences and concerns of contemporary people.

If practical theology's concern with contemporary experience is not to end up with a merely adaptive approach and with asking about *postmodern demands on theology,* we must also become clear about criteria for *theological demands on postmodern life.* The preceding chapters of the present study actually contain at least some initial considerations on such criteria or critical perspectives, but we have not yet put them together into a more comprehensive statement. This is why I will set forth what I call a theology of the life cycle—or, to be more modest, the demand and the parameters for such a theological account.

A first step toward this aim is to formulate some summary observations concerning the contemporary life cycle.

Understanding the Postmodern Life Cycle

As mentioned above, at least for some social scientists it is an open question whether or not there are enough grounds for speaking of a postmodern life cycle. According to those analysts, it is not enough to look only at the philosophical notions of postmodernity and to then assume that peoples' lives or life cycles will have changed more or less in accordance with the theoretical assumptions on postmodernity. Theoretical expectations and the realities of life do not always coincide. Even in postmodernity, life is more complex and more varied than even the most pluralist theory may assume.

Taking the warnings against premature assumptions about a postmodern life cycle seriously, my approach to the topic was inductive by contrasting the ideal description of the *modern life cycle* (which, from a postmodern perspective, has to be considered the traditional life cycle) with the changes and challenges of the *contemporary—possibly postmodern—situation.* This kind of comparison has at least given us an idea of the empirical aspects of postmodern life.

It is, of course, quite impossible to summarize the changes related to the contemporary life cycle here in a few statements, which would amount to condensing the earlier chapters of this book into a few pages. So I will limit myself to a general picture that can highlight some of the core characteristics of this situation.

The main result arising from the consideration of the stages or phases of the life cycle that I have used as my test cases is that the life cycle has indeed changed in a fundamental way. The changes affect not only the experiences that make up the *content* of the various stages of the life cycle but also its very *structure* and *fabric* by giving, for example, rise to new stages like postadolescence or by redefining the existing ones, such as in the case of a Third Age. In this sense, it is justified to speak of a postmodern life cycle in order to distinguish it from its modern counterpart as described, for example, by psychologists like Erik Erikson. The changes that can be observed today affect the meaning of all parts or stages of the life cycle. While we may still speak of childhood, adolescence, adulthood, or old age, all of these terms have clearly assumed a new meaning. At the same time, it is obvious that new and additional periods of the life cycle have emerged and that they are demanding to be acknowledged in their own right: postadolescence, midlife crises, and the various subphases of old age to only mention the more well-known examples. Be it with the new meaning of traditional terms or with the emergence of new stages of the life cycle, it can hardly be doubted that we are, in fact, observing changes of the life cycle that may not easily be captured with the traditional understanding of the modern life cycle. The idea of the modern life cycle still is a backdrop or reference point for helpful comparisons, but it may no longer be considered as an accurate account of today's experience. And it is even less likely to offer us a normative vision amid the crises of contemporary life.

All stages of the life cycle considered above are not just changing by degree. Rather, they have lost some of the key characteristics by which they used to be defined.

- *Childhood* no longer is the relatively quiet time of stability to be experienced and enjoyed in a stable family. Rather, the changes of the family have made childhood a time with many transitions and with new pressures that arise again and again from early on. Literally as well as metaphorically speaking, being a child no longer means living in the safe haven of a home to which one will always look back as the true anchor of one's personal identity.

- Similarly, *adolescence* has ceased to be the time when one develops a lifelong commitment to a clear-cut or at least stable identity and to a worldview that would provide a deep sense of direction in life. In many cases, the experience of being a plural self and of living with plural identities has come to replace such traditional commitments. Plurality has become the inescapable condition for today's adolescence.

• In addition to this, adolescence no longer borders on adulthood but rather on *postadolescence* as a new stage of the life cycle. The transition between adolescence and adulthood has turned into a protracted period of time, with important implications for faith development and for the issue of religious affiliation and disaffiliation.

• Even *adulthood,* which once, even in modern psychology, appeared as the longest and most continuous or stable period within the life cycle, has come into question. None of the modern criteria of being "adult" may be taken for granted anymore. Neither autonomy nor rationality and progressive achievement are still acceptable as true descriptions of adulthood. And at the same time, global economic developments and the media even threaten the status of adulthood itself by not allowing for financial independence or by redefining the value of traditional knowledge that used to be one of the defining privileges of adulthood.

• *Old age* has changed no less. Given the changes within late adulthood and old age, it no longer makes sense to think only of the time of senility or dependence that almost inevitably comes at the end of life. The ideas of a Third Age with new potential and with new exciting possibilities indicates how much the understanding of the period after retirement today can differ from the views maintained only twenty or thirty years ago. The needs of people in the Third Age are not for supportive care. Rather, there now is a clear demand for having a chance to realize some of what one's life did not permit at earlier times.

Given such changes, which have been established by the numerous detailed studies considered in earlier chapters, the question of the postmodern life cycle may now receive at least a somewhat clearer answer. It is true that there are far-reaching changes in the human life cycle. And since these are changes that so clearly differ from the expectations connected to the modern idea of the life cycle, there are indeed good reasons for speaking of a *post*modern life cycle. But in making this statement, the objections against some understandings of postmodernity should also not be overlooked. One of the main objections concerns the identification of postmodernity only by what is lost in the transition from modernity. Often, especially in theology and the church, the loss of a unifying center of norms and values is deplored, and the breakdown of all "master stories" is seen as a threat to the proclamation of the gospel. Yet there is no reason to think of the contemporary situation only as a time of loss, be it in terms of the individual person or be it with respect to church and theology. In many ways, church and theology are facing new challenges, and the postmodern life cycle certainly is not better than its precursors. Yet postmodernity also entails new chances and new potential for human life, which now can be liberated from the narrow visions of rational autonomy and of progressive achievement.

So in some sense, it may be helpful to consider the different terminology that analysts such as Anthony Giddens and Ulrich Beck have suggested in place of the concept of postmodernity.[8] According to them, we should speak of a *second modernity*–a modernity that may also be called *reflexive modernity* in that it includes, even in calling itself modernity, the critical awareness of the shortcomings and of the dark sides of modernity. As opposed to some of the postmodern worldviews, the critical awareness of reflexive modernity is to prevent any kind of depressive nostalgia for the allegedly better times of modernity or even premodernity. Rather, the concept of "reflexive modernization" is to serve as a basis for the continued attempt of counteracting and overcoming the flaws of modernity while still holding on to what is worth preserving of it. To speak of the *life cycle* in the sense of *reflexive modernity* would then imply to consciously hold on to the idea of a meaningful life or of a good life, which is the normative vision built into the modern idea of the life cycle. It would mean to preserve this idea even while realizing, at the same time, that the traditional (that is, "modern") notions of identity and autonomy are highly ambivalent and are much too narrow for being the guiding norms for the life cycle in second modernity. This way of viewing the modern life cycle clearly is in line with the results of my own considerations of the stages of the modern life cycle above. In many cases, be it with modern views of the family and of childhood religion, with adolescent identity formation, or with so-called adult independence, the ambivalence of modern expectations has become obvious. So it makes sense to speak of the need for "reflexive modernization" in respect to the life cycle.

The reflexive and critical perspective on the life cycle is also of immediate interest for practical theology. Many or most of the changes to be observed with the contemporary life cycle also refer to religion or at least have religious implications. Starting in early childhood through adolescence and into adulthood, the substructures of religious nurture, development, and education are being rearranged. So it is easy to see why, for example, many who work with today's children, adolescents, or adults in the church or in related fields of education feel threatened by the far-reaching changes of life structures and orientations. And it is also clear that, as the life cycle is changing, the forms of addressing the people who are moving through this life cycle will also have to change. The postmodern life cycle calls for postmodern approaches in the praxis of the church.

What the perspective of a second–*reflexive*–modernity adds to this picture is a critical and constructive perspective with which this situation can be approached. Rather than deploring the losses of postmodernity and rather than becoming desperate with its pluriformities, this perspective may encourage us to ask about the *possibilities* of the postmodern life cycle. In my understanding, it must be the task of a contemporary practical theology to become a *practical theology of reflexive modernization* and to serve as a *mediator* and *midwife* for those possibilities.

In order to illustrate this understanding, I conclude this section by connecting it with some of the considerations from my analysis of the changing shape of adulthood (in chapter 5). As pointed out there, modernity has been especially productive in terms of images of adulthood. In some ways, we may say that modernity itself was closely connected with the proud hope of the Enlightenment, that humanity had finally reached adulthood and maturity. Modern adulthood is often identified with autonomy, independence, and rationality. This understanding also affects religion, which is limited to the role of supporting rational autonomy, especially in the realm of ethics. And even more, religion does not have a proper place in modern adulthood. In the meantime, however, the modern idea of adulthood has itself been challenged as an ideology. It never included those who were prevented from becoming fully autonomous, independent, and rational. And in addition to this, the modern understanding of adulthood cannot cover the varieties of postmodern life, be it with new lifestyles or with new interests in religion and spirituality. Here, with the idea of modern adulthood, the postmodern challenges are by no means only detrimental. Rather, they include healthy possibilities, and they provide a new openness at exactly those points where the modern life cycle tended to become suffocating.

Practical Theology between Modernity and Postmodernity

The traditional or, more accurately, the original understanding of practical theology as an academic discipline is closely tied to the emergence of modernity in the eighteenth century. When Friedrich Schleiermacher, who often is considered the father of practical theology, and his contemporaries designed the project of practical theology as a separate branch or subdiscipline of theology, they worked against the background of the challenges posed by modernity and the Enlightenment. One of the main challenges was to show that religion and the church were not just remnants of the Dark Ages of premodernity but that they have a meaningful future role to play.[9] This is why Schleiermacher attempted to show that human existence is incomplete and impoverished if religion is not given its proper place in human life. Moreover, he argues that the church can be conceived of as an institution for the religious communication that is needed for enabling the individual persons to express their religious feelings and, in turn, to be stimulated by the preaching and teaching of the church. In all of this, the main challenge consisted in the sharp tension between the Christian tradition on the one hand and modern culture on the other. This is why practical theology was designed as a mediator—a mediator between tradition and modernity, between religion and rationality, and between the church and the life worlds of modernity.[10]

Given the close relationship between modernity and the emergence of practical theology as a new theological discipline, it is obvious why postmodernity intrinsically implies a fundamental challenge for practical theology. If we have actually moved beyond the scope of modernity—and the changes of the modern life cycle may be taken as an empirical indication of this move—the task of mediating between the Christian tradition and modernity is also affected. This is why the issue of postmodernity is so pressing for practical theology. It actually confronts this discipline with the question of its future existence and also with the need to reconsider its mediating task.

Is there still a need for mediation between the Christian tradition and contemporary experience once we have moved beyond modernity? In my understanding, the answer must clearly be "yes." The characteristics of postmodernity that are described in the literature—pluralization, individualization, the end of all "master stories," and so forth—indicate that the move beyond modernity or, to again use this terminology, the arrival of a second modernity, does not mean that contemporary culture and society are returning to the premodern unity of Christianity, culture, and society.[11] Even if the contemporary situation includes, as will be pointed out later in this chapter, a certain return to religion, it is not institutionalized religion in the sense of the Christian church that has received renewed attention. Rather, it is spirituality in the sense of a personal religious interest without institutional affiliation. Consequently, the future role of practical theology may still be described with the term "mediator." What has changed, however, is the polarity that makes theological mediation necessary, but the task of mediation itself has not disappeared. In my understanding, the task of mediation now refers to the tensions arising in the transition between modernity and postmodernity or between first modernity and second modernity.

In this understanding, practical theology as mediator is related to a temporal and cultural transition from first to second modernity. We are talking about the conflictual sequence of two different epochs or of two different cultures, and the task of practical theology as mediator is to support the church in this transition as well as to offer guidance to a wider public. This task necessarily also includes a social dimension of practical theology. Given the impact of pluralization, individualization, distance from institutions, and so forth, practical theology can only do its job of mediation by facilitating productive connections between church, individual religion, and the public.

If we consider again, for the sake of being more specific, the changing stages of the life cycle mentioned above, it seems obvious to me that practical theology as mediator must tap into what we have called the potential of postmodernity vis-à-vis the procrustean bed of the modern life cycle. But it has also become clear that we cannot accept, let alone uncritically praise, whatever calls itself postmodern. Rather, we need a careful and critical examination of the diverse changes between modernity and postmodernity in order to identify what may really be called a potential and what rather should be seen as detrimental. To put it into one sentence: Support for helpful postmodern developments but also critical resistance to what cannot be accepted of postmodernity—this is the substantial work of practical theology as mediator between the first and second modernity.

In a further step, this general statement must be related to religion—especially to the relationship between church, individual religion, and the public.[12] Again, we encounter an ambivalent situation. Modernity has worked toward separating the different fields of religion. The public realm was conceived of as secular or, if not so, as undergirded by some type of civil religion. The religion of the individual person was confined to the private realm (religious privatization). Consequently, the distance among church, the public realm, and individual life was not only increased empirically but it was turned, at least in part, into a permanent situation guarded by legal as well as political principles. In this view, the public realm must be secular, individual persons must keep their religious "preferences" to themselves as long as they are in public, and the church is not to interfere with this situation of clear-cut separation.

From social scientific as well as from theological analyses of postmodernity, it may be seen that the interplay among church, individual religion, and the public realm does not stay the same with postmodernity. There are new chances for religion to claim a stronger role in public life, for example, through the various political movements that are motivated by religion.[13] Yet at the same time, it is difficult to see how religion may actually play this role if religion, for the most part, is increasingly individualized and privatized. Also, the position of the church clearly becomes weaker if more and more people see no connection between their personal faith and the teachings of the church. This is why the work of practical theology as mediator must include a social dimension. In being a midwife for the religious potential of second modernity, it must mediate among church, individual religion, and the public realm.

In this case, mediation means building connections and making voices heard. As theologians concern themselves with the postmodern life cycle, they are showing a new willingness to listen to the people and to become open to their actual life experiences. This clearly is a first step toward strengthening the relationship between the church and the individual person. The next step will be to devise additional strategies—be it in preaching or teaching, in liturgy or in pastoral care—strategies that address the needs of those who have to find their way through the postmodern life cycle.

In some ways, mediating between the church and the individual person has always been the task of practical theology. The other tension, however—the tension between church and public life or between individual religion and the public—has received far less attention. Yet the task is clear in this respect as well. If the church is to claim a stronger role in public life, it must itself become what may be called a *public community*—a community that brings together, in a convincing manner, the strength of forming communal bonds as they arise from a particular faith and from a particular ethos, and the universal responsibility for the common good of all citizens and of all human beings.

To put it in a nutshell: The task of practical theology in its social dimension includes the threefold focus on church, individual religion, and the public, as well as on the dynamic interrelationships among all three of them. So practical theology, as I understand it, must be a theological discipline with a theoretical horizon that is much wider than the traditional definitions of this discipline, which relate it only to pastoral work within the church. I clearly affirm the ecclesial focus of practical theology because religious institutions are necessary. But we must also extend practical theology to refer to individual life and to the role of religion in the public sphere.[14]

If practical theology is to fulfill this task, it is in need of clear theological criteria. These criteria must enable it to critically assess the transitional process from first to second modernity, and they must also offer guidance for the mediating work of practical theology in the dynamic interrelationship of church, individual religion, and the public. In order to show what this means, I will again refer to the life cycle by asking how a theological perspective on the life cycle may be articulated.

The relationship between practical theology and postmodernity is in need of a more detailed discussion. The present chapter certainly is not meant to be exhaustive. It is focused on the question of what postmodernity means for our understanding of the tasks of practical theology. Postmodernity does not imply the end of practical theology as mediation, but it makes it mandatory to reassess and to redesign the ways in which this mediation is to be carried out.

Do we need a new paradigm for practical theology? The reference to a "new paradigm" is always ambivalent if it refers to the present in which one lives. Actually, if taken seriously, the concept of paradigm as developed by Thomas Kuhn[15] implies that those who are working within a certain paradigm are not aware of it. The paradigm is operative behind their backs. It is nothing that can be introduced intentionally. So my point is not about the term "paradigm" and my plea is not for an intentional change of paradigms (which would be a contradiction in terms). My plea is for a practical theology facing up to the challenges of contemporary life, which, in important respects, is no longer "modern" in the traditional sense.

Toward a Theology of the Life Cycle

The step that I want to take in this final section confronts us with a somewhat paradoxical task. On the one hand, in the interest of the criteria needed for practical theology in the transition between modernity and postmodernity, theology now must be our starting point—or, more exactly, we need a theological perspective on the life cycle. Yet on the other hand, such a theological perspective is not readily available. To my knowledge, there is no publication available from systematic theology or from theological ethics that would offer a "theology of the life cycle," at least not from recent times.[16] Of course, there are accounts from pastoral theology and from Christian education that deal with parts or aspects of the life cycle for purposes of counseling and education.[17] But with very few exceptions—most notably James Loder's book on *Human Development in Theological Perspective*[18]—they do not offer a comprehensive theological perspective on the life cycle as a whole. And even Loder's approach, on which I will draw implicitly, does not focus on the postmodern life cycle but rather is meant as a critical dialogue with the psychology of human development independent of the life cycle in modernity or postmodernity.

Given the enormous attention that the modern life cycle has received in the second half of the twentieth century, and given the challenges that postmodernity is setting before us, it is probably not unfair to say that theology has not done its homework in this respect. It is clearly not enough to rely only on theological doctrines and principles that have not entered the dialogue with the experiences connected to the postmodern life cycle. If theology is to offer guidance and support in the transition from first to second modernity, a theology of the life cycle is an indispensable presupposition for the critical discernment and mediation of practical theology.

So what are we to do in this situation? It is clear what we need, but what we need is not available. It will certainly not be possible to fill this gap in the last section of this book, and I will not pretend that I am in the position to offer a comprehensive model. What is possible, however, is to set forth a number of key points or perspectives that, at least in my understanding, identify the decisive issues to be included in a theology of the life cycle. And by putting together some of the theological understandings developed in earlier chapters of this book, we can at least work toward a first outline for a theology of the life cycle, which can be used as a scaffolding for future work.

The task of a theology of the life cycle is to set forth a theological interpretation of the life cycle and of its different stages. This interpretation must include answers to at least three questions, which are of key importance to the people moving through this life cycle.

- What aspects of the *Christian faith* are of special importance at the different stages? How does this faith address the issues of different phases of the life cycle?

- What *ethical guidelines* does this faith include with respect to different ages, stages, or phases of life?

- How is *religious communication* possible vis-à-vis the postmodern challenges of the pluralization, individualization, and privatization of religion?

All three questions stand for perspectives or for demands that theology raises over against the postmodern life cycle. At the same time, they indicate where theological work has to go beyond its traditional understanding if it is to be in touch with postmodern life.

(1) First, I take up the perspective of *faith.* How is the Christian understanding of faith related to the postmodern life cycle? It has been one of the central achievements of practical theology in the second half of the twentieth century to identify images and stories that correlate most exactly with the specific experiences of different stages of the life cycle. Such theological correlations most often make use of Erikson's model, which indicates that they actually refer to the *modern life cycle.* By summarizing and synthesizing the different models that practical theologians and Christian educators have set forth in the literature, we can draw up a correlational chart that looks something like this:[19]

Crises of the (Modern) Life Cycle	Religious/Christian Symbols
basic trust vs. mistrust	the numinous (God, mother, goddesses), the (lost) paradise, and the hope for the kingdom of God
autonomy vs. shame and doubt	good and evil, grace, obedience and exodus, symbols of eating and drinking
initiative vs. guilt	loving and punishing father Godhead, sin and redemption, repentance
industry vs. inferiority	vocation/calling, God's creation and responsibility, works
identity vs. identity confusion	God's solidarity (in suffering), alienation and redemption
intimacy vs. isolation	community, themes of christology
generativity vs. stagnation	creation, vocation/calling, care for the future
integrity vs. despair	the holy, the last thing

This summary chart obviously is based on the *modern* life cycle, not only because it incorporates Erikson's stages but also because the conflicts and ambivalence connected to the postmodern situation are missing. And the same is true for the new possibilities that this situation includes according to the evaluations of my own study presented above. This does not mean that the correlational efforts contained in the chart have become worthless. As we have seen at many points, the changes to be observed with our contemporary situation have not taken away the expectations connected to the modern life cycle altogether. But there can be no doubt that the traditional (modern) crises of the life cycle do not sufficiently capture the experiences of contemporary people anymore. Consequently, the task of a theology of the postmodern life cycle consists of recasting such correlations in the light of the contemporary changes of this life cycle.

The task of redrawing the chart above in order to make it fit the postmodern life cycle is complex and demanding, and I think it would be premature to actually produce a new chart. But it makes sense to indicate the principles for the construction of such a new correlational chart by drawing on the chapters above, and to specify at least a number of examples for which religious or Christian symbols could become important in the present situation. For the sake of a simplified description, I will only refer to childhood, adolescence, and adulthood.

Childhood: The symbols suggested in the *modern* chart above are often geared to the experience of growing up with mother and father, of being raised with clear and demanding educational standards, and of struggling with the sometimes overwhelming authority of the adult generation. What seems to be less in view is the experience of growing up with only one parent, the absence of the father even in a two-parent household, the lack of clear standards and expectations, and the vulnerability of parents or educators who are puzzled by the question of what authority they should use after all. These *postmodern* experiences clearly lead to an entire set of crises that are different from those expected in the model of the modern life cycle. Different problems are becoming important, like issues of trustworthiness vis-à-vis parents who turn out not to be trustworthy, the experience of loss and abandonment, the need for hope and for guidance. These themes are also present in the Christian tradition, but symbols or stories must now be selected and be presented in line with what have become typical conflicts of contemporary childhood.

The symbol of the good shepherd (Lk. 15:1–7), for example, certainly remains important, but it can also take on new meaning for those who have never had a chance to experience a truly shepherding parent. Or to mention another example, the story of Jonah being lost on a journey and of having to survive a state of limbo certainly will be attractive to children who themselves feel that they have gotten lost somewhere along their families' journeys.

Another set of problems has to do with the tension between belonging and openness described in chapter 2. If a pluralism of religions and worldviews has become a reality for many children from early experiences, they also need symbols and stories to support them in sorting out the potentially disorienting effects.

Adolescence: The crises and conflicts addressed in the *modern* chart reflect experiences of oppression and of liberation, that is, of a self that has to struggle to free itself from overwhelming social expectations and from predefined social roles. Again, while issues of oppression and liberation remain important, the specifically *postmodern* exposure to pluralization and individualization is lacking in this modern interpretation. The challenges of plural selves and plural identities described in chapter 3 include the experience of incompleteness and of discontinuity. Vis-à-vis the danger of fragmentation that this experience entails, the positive acceptance of the fragmentary character of the human self as an expression of human finitude can give the young person a new and encouraging sense of selfhood. This is especially true if the acceptance of one's limits is not due only to resignation or frustration with oneself but if it comes also in response to the experience of God's love and acceptance, which are not based on personal achievements. This is why I pointed to the crucial importance of the teaching of the justification by faith, which means exactly this–that human selfhood is not an achievement but, in the first place, a gift from God. And the insight into the deeply relational character of human existence implied by this teaching can help young people in overcoming the widespread individualistic views of the self and in finding a sense of direction vis-à-vis the relativism such views imply.

Adulthood: I intentionally do not distinguish here between (proper) adulthood and old age. This distinction on which the *modern* chart is based has turned out to be ideological in that it limits the status of being truly adult to those in full possession of autonomy and independence. This tendency is paralleled by associating work-related symbols such as vocation to the age of adulthood, and symbols such as the "last things" to old age. The *postmodern* experience challenges us, as shown in chapters 5 and 6, to thoroughly rethink such expectations and to make space for new understandings of adulthood, as well as old age.

For what used to be called (proper) adulthood, we need symbols that can support alternative visions of maturity by reconciling the idea of adulthood with dependence and relatedness, with weakness, and with emotional or playful attitudes. In other words, if our understanding of what it means to be truly adult were to be broadened, the characteristics excluded or suppressed by modernity would, out of necessity, be reemphasized and reintegrated.

The situation is somewhat different with what I called, drawing on Peter Laslett's work in chapter 6, the Third Age, which used to be considered as late adulthood. Here, the emphasis must be on symbols and models of people who, in spite of their not being adolescents anymore, still found the courage and energy to start something new. The biblical archetypes for this certainly are Abraham's relocating to Canaan and Moses' leading the exodus, but there also are women like Miriam (Ex. 15:20) whose importance has recently been rediscovered.

Much more could be said about the meaning of faith in different postmodern contexts of life. Yet the principles that can lead to a more comprehensive account are clear enough. We need religious or Christian symbols that speak to the postmodern experience as opposed to modernity, that offer critical guidance to people vis-à-vis agnosticism and relativism, and that support the efforts of making use of new possibilities implicit in the postmodern situation. In this way, the attempt of correlating the Christian tradition and contemporary experiences is carried out in the sense of what I called the midwife function of practical theology.

Yet as important as the correlational task will be for the future of practical theology, we still have to go one step farther. The idea of correlating the Christian tradition with contemporary experiences of the life cycle actually includes a presupposition that, in postmodernity, can no longer be taken for granted. This presupposition refers to the fundamental question: Why should we even think of such correlations? If postmodernity means the end of all "master stories," it could also mean that a theological perspective on the life cycle is simply not needed any longer.

At this point, a theology of the life cycle has to go beyond individual correlations and to establish itself on the level of fundamental anthropology. In other words, a theology of the life cycle has to show that the question of faith is actually built into the human life cycle as such and therefore is not dependent on the experience of modernity. Birth and death, trust and anxiety, autonomy and dependence, identity and the denial of selfhood—all these experiences are potentially religious experiences. They carry with them a deep demand for ultimate answers—a demand that obviously is not only stated by theologians but is experienced by many people. Postmodernity may be the end of all "master stories," but it clearly does not put an end to the questions of faith as they arise from the life cycle.

Summarizing the first task of a theology of the life cycle, we can distinguish between two different aspects—on the one hand, to bring into conversation with each other the Christian tradition and the experiences of the postmodern life cycle in the sense of correlation, and, on the other, to show on the level of fundamental anthropology how faith and the life cycle belong together even beyond modernity.

(2) The second task of a theology of the life cycle refers to the perspective of *Christian ethics*. This perspective refers to two different aspects or levels that must be addressed: the level of a *responsible individual life* and the level of *responsibility for the life cycle.*

Responsible individual life: This level concerns the question of how the individual person should live and act. Where Christian ethics and practical theology have addressed this question, they have done so in terms of moral guidelines for finding one's way through the life cycle and also in terms of the virtues that might be helpful and important in individual life. On the whole, there have not been many attempts, however, to relate the perspective of Christian ethics to the various stages of the life cycle in a comprehensive manner. This is why we turn again, for the last time in this book, to Erik Erikson, whose work on the modern life cycle also includes important ethical aspects.

Erikson often refers to ethical aspects as part of his view of the life cycle and of the developmental tasks connected to it. His most comprehensive treatment of the topic can be found in his essay "A Schedule of Virtues."[20] There he develops an interpretation of his eight stages of the life cycle, which focuses on the virtues that should be developed at each stage. His descriptions are summarized in the overview below.

It is interesting to note that many of these virtues come from the Christian tradition or can at least be interpreted in a Christian sense. This is especially true for *hope* and *fidelity*, but it also applies to *love, care,* and *wisdom.* This makes this chart of ethical perspectives in correlation to the stages of the life cycle a valuable potential contribution to a theology of the life cycle.

Yet it is also easy to see that we have to go beyond Erikson's modern scheme if we want to address the postmodern life cycle. Taking up Erikson's terminology of virtues, we must add new virtues that correspond to the challenges of postmodern life described in the

Stages of the life cycle	Virtues
Infancy	hope
Early childhood	will
Childhood	purpose
School age	competence
Adolescence	fidelity
Young adulthood	love
Adulthood	care
Old age	wisdom

previous chapters. For example, Erikson's scheme does not foresee a clear place for virtues like critical discernment vis-à-vis pluralism or for the dialogical and relational abilities that are called for by the need to overcome contemporary individualism. In a similar vein, the virtue of responsibility has rightfully received new attention in feminist psychology.[21] Such examples indicate the need to have a fresh look at the ethical tasks connected to an individual's life under the conditions of postmodernity. There is a need for ethical guidelines and virtues, even in postmodernity. Yet the ethical challenge runs deeper, and this is why a Christian ethics of the life cycle has to address a second level—ethical issues not only *within* the life cycle but responsibility *for* the life cycle itself.

Responsibility for the life cycle: The starting point for assuming responsibility for the life cycle is the insight repeated over and over in the chapters above, that the life cycle—actually any life cycle, postmodern or not—is not just a natural given. As has been pointed out above, the shape of the life cycle is thoroughly dependent on influences from culture and society. If this is true, the life cycle itself can, and from my point of view also must, be seen as a field of ethical responsibility. Since the life cycle is not an anthropological given that never changes, we ourselves become responsible for how the life cycle is shaped and what structures are given to it.

At first glance, it may not sound very plausible to identify this kind of responsibility as a key task of Christian ethics. In modernity, the main concern between theology and a psychology of the life cycle seemed to be how theology and the church can become more sensitive to the different ages and stages of the human life cycle that they want to address. And like many other modern topics, this question has not lost its importance. It is still quite essential, for example, that Christian educators learn to really understand children in their unique ways of approaching the world. Yet at the same time, the postmodern life cycle makes us painfully aware of how flexible and how contingent all ages and stages of the life cycle really are. Childhood today and the childhood of our grandparents have little in common, and the lives of our children will probably again be very different from ours. This is why the postmodern life cycle poses a different and additional challenge to theology—the responsibility for shaping the life cycle itself. What does this mean?

To state it once more: The process through which the life cycle is changing is not a natural given. It is the result of social, political, and cultural processes, and this implies that there are decisions involved—decisions that are made at various levels and that together lead to the changes of the life cycle. There are the decisions of individuals, who make their choices for certain lifestyles or careers. There are decisions of churches, which make policies, for example, in respect to supporting or not supporting families. And there are decisions in politics, which affect the social and economic parameters of the life cycle in all of society.

All these decisions play into what finally appears as the given ("natural") shape and structure of the life cycle. The challenge that theological ethics puts before us today is how such decisions can be made in a responsible manner and in accordance with Christian views of the person and of society. In other words, the new flexibility and pluriformity also open up new possibilities for consciously shaping the life cycle, or more modestly, they make us aware of how policy decisions will inevitably influence the shape of the life cycle.

Given this situation, there is an increasingly pressing need for theology and the church to become clear about what forms of childhood, adolescence, adulthood, and so forth are healthy and humane from their perspective. This is why a theology of the life cycle has become an immensely important task, not only for responsible life within the life cycle but also in order to claim a Christian responsibility for the future shape of the life cycle.

(3) The third question that a theology of the life cycle must address—the question of *religious communication*—is of a somewhat different nature. It is less obvious than the first two questions of faith and of responsibility. Why does the question of religious communication arise in this context?

Again we are confronted with a specific challenge of postmodern life. Religious communication becomes extremely difficult and diffuse in postmodernity. This is because of the two interrelated processes of the pluralization and the individualization of religion, which, in extreme cases, may mean that a language may not even be available that would be suitable for purposes of religious communication. When everything about religion is left to the individual to pursue from early years, there often is no chance for children or youth to acquire such a language. Faith or religion then remains a purely private matter pertaining only to inner feelings that cannot be shared with others. Even where this is not the case and where such a language is still acquired through education, religious discourse in public becomes difficult because, once religion is treated as a purely private matter, religious language is seen as limited to a religious community. And indeed, the traditional forms of Christian language have rarely been developed for the purposes of public dialogue on religious issues. This is one of the reasons why such issues are often excluded from the public realm. Of course, religion may still be addressed in legal or political terms or from the perspective of the social sciences. But in all these cases, public dialogue is *about* religion, but it certainly is not a *religious* dialogue expressive of different faiths.

In my understanding, this situation is detrimental in several respects. First, it is detrimental in that a whole dimension of human life—the religious dimension of the life cycle—is not given full access to human communication. Second, it is detrimental to society in that there is no meaningful public exchange on matters of ultimate meaning. And third, it is detrimental for the church in that any public communication on faith and religion becomes more difficult, even in the limited public of a particular church. Consequently, a theology of the life cycle must include the task of designing models for religious communication—models that work within the church but that are also viable for a wider public.

Why must such models be designed in the context of the life cycle? In my understanding, there are at least two important reasons for this need. The first reason refers to the educational and developmental prerequisites for religious communication. This kind of communication presupposes certain abilities, such as knowing the appropriate language, being able to express and to explain one's own faith in such a way that others who do not share it can make sense of it, taking the perspective of the other, and so forth. Such abilities must be developed and acquired at appropriate times in life, which is why a theology of the life cycle should inform us about the dialogical or communicative learning tasks related to the respective stages of the life cycle.

The second reason for including the perspective of religious communication within a theology of the life cycle has once more to do with the challenges of postmodernity. To the degree that the postmodern pluralization leads to religious individualism and privatism, theology and the church must have a strong interest in overcoming such tendencies. The Christian faith, by its very nature, cannot be reduced to an individualistic and private matter. It refers to, and it deeply respects, every individual person in his or her own right. But it can only do so by claiming a public role in society. To develop a theology of the life cycle does not mean that theology should only be attentive to individual or personal concerns. Rather, such a theology is itself of public concern and importance, especially for the inhabitants of postmodernity.

Faith, Christian ethics, and religious communication indicate three directions in which the task of developing a theology of the life cycle should be pursued in more detail. And it is also clear that what we need is a theology of the postmodern life cycle, a theology for our contemporary situation. This theology must be able to look in two directions—in the direction of postmodern life and its demands on theology and the church, but also in the direction of Christian theology and its demands on postmodern life.

Still a Life Cycle?

At the end of this book, I want to return to a question that first came up in the introduction and that readers may feel deserves a still more explicit and definitive answer than I have given so far. This book carries the title, *The Postmodern Life Cycle.* Its focus is on the many changes of the various stages of the modern life cycle, in childhood and adolescence, but also in adulthood. We have observed far-reaching transformations that clearly affect the traditional understanding of such ages or stages. And we have also seen that new stages have emerged, such as postadolescence between adolescence and adulthood, and the Third Age between modern adulthood and old age. Does all of this lead to the conclusion that we should drop the whole idea or image of a life cycle in order to replace it with a symbol of discontinuity and pluriformity?

Considering the empirical evidence compiled in the chapters above, one could probably justify this conclusion. Yet before accepting this point of view and before calling postmodernity the end of the outdated model of the life cycle, we have to consider another question in order to avoid premature consequences that are based on mistaken assumptions about earlier times. Is it really true that modernity did, or at least could, offer the experience of a life as a continuous and meaningful pattern? Did modernity, in fact, give people the opportunity for wholeness and completion? Posing such questions almost means answering them. It has become commonplace and all too well-known that modernity was anything but an ideal time for experiences of meaningful wholeness and completion. Rather, from the beginning, many people living in modernity were never given a chance to really aspire, let alone achieve, for example, the ideals of adulthood described above. Autonomy, rationality, financial independence, careers, and professional success were never an option for many people because they were lacking personal abilities or the appropriate social and financial resources to proceed in this direction. And in addition to this, we can learn, for example, from much of twentieth-century literature how far away people's real experiences were from the ideals of wholeness, completion, and a meaningful life. Just think of the characters literally beset with the threat of absurdity that are so vividly described in the novels of many twentieth-century authors—from Franz Kafka to Jean-Paul Sartre or from Hermann Hesse to Douglas Coupland. Most often, the lives of their characters end up in shambles. If anything, it is the image of fragments that fits their life but never that of a rounded figure ("cycle") or gestalt. On the whole, it seems fair to say that wholeness and completion were no less rare exceptions in modernity than they obviously are in postmodernity. Postmodern interpreters have, perhaps, become more outspoken about this experience, but this does not mean that things have really changed with respect to the experience of failing to live up to the expectations of wholeness and completion.

But what are we to conclude from this observation? What does it mean for the idea or image of the life cycle if it was no less removed from reality in modernity than it is in postmodernity? In this situation, two rather contradictory conclusions appear to be plausible.

(1) According to the first of them, we could say that postmodernity has finally made us aware of what always has been true, that is, of the highly ideological and distortive nature of ideals and images that society or religion imposes on life. In chapter 1, we had occasion to consider different images of the family, which can be interpreted in this sense of society valuing or even prescribing certain models of family life and making people adapt to such expectations. Additional examples examined in chapter 5 concern the modern image of the adult as an autonomous, rational, and independent individual or, in chapter 6, the image of senile person in old age. In such cases, the postmodern critique of ideology does indeed apply. Ideological images contained in the model of the life cycle must be exposed and changed. And this kind of critical analysis has to be accepted as an important step toward more humane forms of life. To the degree that distortive ideals can be challenged, the realities of life receive a better chance of being accepted rather than having to be disguised for the sake of social acceptability. This has to be appreciated as one of the liberating experiences connected to postmodernity. And to the degree that the idea of a life cycle draws upon such mistaken ideals, we have to

challenge and to criticize this idea. A critical view of the model of the life cycle should therefore remain with us in the future as well.

(2) Yet what comes after having become critical of the existing models of the life cycle? Can we really live without having some image of wholeness and completion? Would this not amount to giving ourselves up completely to the unpredictable vicissitudes of postmodern flexibility and discontinuity? As we have also come to see in the chapters of the present study, this kind of life is not in line with the visions of Christian theology. This is the point at which the second possible reaction to the realization of the unreal character of the life cycle comes into play, that is, the possibility of viewing the life cycle as a vision or longing, which cannot be judged by only comparing it to what life really looks like at a given time. The vision or idea of the life cycle is as far away from the modern experience as it is from the postmodern one. In either case, the reality of people's lives was and still is quite different from what this vision entails for it. But to the degree that this vision is expressive of people's longings for a meaningful life that arrives, at least to some degree, at something like wholeness and completion, it cannot be criticized for not being in line with reality. Such criticism would only be legitimate to the degree that the idea of the life cycle becomes itself one-sided and oppressive, for example, by burdening people with the expectation of having to meet the expectations of financial success. But in themselves, ideals or visions can never be criticized for their distance from reality. Otherwise, they could never fulfill their role of challenging reality and of keeping alive the hope for a better life or for a different reality.

Viewing the life cycle as such a vision, which keeps alive our hopes for a better reality, again makes clear how important it is to consider it from the perspective of a theology of the life cycle. If it is true that the life cycle mainly confronts us with ideal images, longings, and normative visions, a theology is nothing foreign to this idea. Rather than being a theological intrusion into the field of the social sciences or of psychology, such a theology operates exactly at the same level as these nontheological disciplines.

Finally, calling the life cycle a vision does not mean that the differences between modernity and postmodernity do not matter anymore. While it is true that the model of the life cycle has never described a reality in the strict empirical sense, and while it is also true that, by their very nature, visions always transcend reality, modernity and postmodernity still produce their own kinds of specific contradictions to the ideal model of the life cycle. This is why we do not need only a theology of the life cycle but also a theology of the *postmodern life cycle.* And only by looking into the realities of people's contemporary experiences can church and theology become able to face up to the challenges of postmodern life.

Notes

Introduction

[1]To mention only a few of their publications: Richard R. Osmer, *A Teachable Spirit: Recovering the Teaching Office in the Church* (Louisville: Westminster/John Knox Press, 1990); Don S. Browning, *Generative Man: Psychoanalytic Perspectives* (New York: Delta, 1975); idem, *A Fundamental Practical Theology: Descriptive and Strategic Proposals* (Minneapolis: Fortress Press, 1991); James W. Fowler, *Weaving the New Creation: Stages of Faith and the Public Church* (San Francisco: HarperSanFrancisco, 1991); idem, *Faithful Change: The Personal and Public Challenges of Postmodern Life* (Nashville: Abingdon Press, 1996).

[2]Three of the chapters of the book have been published in a preliminary form elsewhere. See Friedrich Schweitzer, "Religious Affiliation and Disaffiliation in Late Adolescence and Early Adulthood: The Impact of a Neglected Period of Life," in *Joining and Leaving Religion: Research Perspectives*, ed. Leslie J. Francis and Yaacov J. Katz (Leominster: Gracewing, 2000), 87–101; idem, "Church, Individual Religion, Public Responsibility: Images of Faith between Modern and Postmodern Adulthood," *Princeton Seminary Bulletin* 21 (2000): 287–300; idem, "Practical Theology and Postmodern Life: Do We Need a New Paradigm?" *International Journal of Practical Theology* 5 (2001): 169–83.

Chapter 1:The Religious Demands of Postmodern Life

[1]See Jean-François Lyotard, *The Postmodern Condition: A Report on Knowledge* (Minneapolis: Univ. of Minnesota Press, 1984).

[2]Deutsches Jugendinstitut, ed., *Was für Kinder. Aufwachsen in Deutschland. Ein Handbuch* (Munich: Kösel, 1993), 62–72.

[3]This notion has been introduced in this sense by modern systems theory; see Niklas Luhmann and Karl-Eberhard Schorr, *Reflexionsprobleme im Erziehungssystem* (Stuttgart: Klett, 1979), 277ff., especially in regard to modern education.

[4]See Ulrich Beck, *Risk Society: Towards a New Modernity* (London: Sage, 1992).

[5]See, for example, Werner Helsper, "Das 'postmoderne Selbst'–ein neuer Subjekt- und Jugend-Mythos? Reflexionen anhand religiöser jugendlicher Orientierungen," in *Identitätsarbeit heute. Klassische und aktuelle Perspektiven der Identitätsforschung*, ed. Heiner Keupp and Renate Höfer (Frankfurt am Main: Suhrkamp, 1997), 174–206.

[6]Elisabeth Beck-Gernsheim, *Was kommt nach der Familie? Einblicke in neue Lebensformen* (Munich: Beck, 1998), 17.

[7]Harvey Cox, *Secular City: Urbanization and Secularization in Theological Perspective* (New York: Macmillan, 1965).

[8]Harvey Cox, *Religion in the Secular City: Toward a Postmodern Theology* (New York: Simon & Schuster, 1984).

[9]For a discussion, see Peter L. Berger, ed., *The Desecularization of the World: Resurgent Religion and World Politics* (Grand Rapids: Eerdmans, 1999).

[10]For the development of church membership in the United States, see Wade Clark Roof and William McKinney, *American Mainline Religion: Its Changing Shape and Future* (New Brunswick: Rutgers University Press, 1987); Robert Wuthnow, *The Restructuring of American Religion: Society and Faith Since World War II* (Princeton: Princeton University Press, 1988); for Germany, see Klaus Engelhardt et al., eds., *Fremde Heimat Kirche. Die dritte EKD–Erhebung über Kirchenmitgliedschaft* (Gütersloh: Gütersloher Verlagshaus, 1997).

[11]See, for example, Wade Clark Roof, *Spiritual Marketplace: Baby Boomers and the Remaking of American Religion* (Princeton: Princeton University Press, 1999); Diana Eck, *A New Religious America: How a "Christian Country" Has Now Become the World's Most Religiously Diverse Nation* (San Francisco: HarperSanFrancisco, 2001). For an earlier

and more popular account, see Malise Ruthven, *The Divine Supermarket: Shopping for God in America* (New York: W. Morrow, 1989).

[12]Peter L. Berger, *The Heretical Imperative: Contemporary Possibilities of Religious Affirmation* (Garden City, New York: Anchor, 1979).

[13]For a helpful introduction, see Peter L. Berger, Brigitte Berger, and Hansfried Kellner, *The Homeless Mind: Modernization and Consciousness* (New York: Vintage, 1974), 65ff.

[14]José Casanova, *Public Religions in the Modern World* (Chicago: Univ. of Chicago Press, 1994); Peter Beyer, *Religion and Globalization* (London: Sage, 1994); see also Berger, *Desecularization.*

[15]Samuel P. Huntington, *The Clash of Civilizations and the Remaking of World Order* (New York: Simon & Schuster, 1996).

[16]Roland Robertson, *Globalization: Social Theory and Global Culture* (London: Sage, 1992); Beyer, *Religion and Globalization;* Anthony Giddens, *Modernity and Self-Identity: Self and Society in the Late Modern Age* (Stanford: Stanford University Press, 1991).

[17]For a good collection, see Kieran Flanagan and Peter C. Jupp, eds., *Postmodernity, Sociology and Religion* (New York: St. Martin's, 1996).

[18]Helpful summaries may be found in David Harvey, *The Postmodern Condition* (Oxford: Blackwell, 1989); Wolfgang Welsch, *Unsere postmoderne Moderne* (Weinheim: VCH, 1988).

[19]For a discussion on methodology, see David Tracy, *Blessed Rage for Order: The New Pluralism in Theology* (Chicago: Chicago University Press, new ed. 1996); Don S. Browning, ed., *Practical Theology* (San Francisco: Harper & Row, 1983); idem, *A Fundamental Practical Theology: Descriptive and Strategic Proposals* (Minneapolis: Fortress Press, 1991); Friedrich Schweitzer and Johannes A. van der Ven, eds., *Practical Theology— International Perspectives* (Frankfurt am Main: P. Lang, 1999).

[20]To mention just one example, see Anthony C. Tiselton, *Interpreting God and the Postmodern Self: On Meaning, Manipulation and Promise* (Grand Rapids: Eerdmans, 1995). He is interested in questions similar to mine. His approach, however, is fairly different. As a systematic theologian, he focuses his study on the philosophical and theological tradition without special reference to contemporary life or the life cycle as the background of the "postmodern self."

[21]See Harvey, *Postmodern Condition*, and Welsch, *Moderne.*

[22]For a detailed account, see Lawrence Jacob Friedmann, *Identity's Architect: A Biography of Erik H. Erikson* (New York: Scribner, 1999).

[23]For the best accounts on Erikson and religion, see J. Eugene Wright, *Erikson: Identity and Religion* (New York: Seabury, 1982); Hetty Zock, *A Psychology of Ultimate Concern: Erik H. Erikson's Contribution to the Psychology of Religion* (Amsterdam and Atlanta: Rodopi, 1990).

[24]Robert Kegan, *In Over Our Heads: The Mental Demands of Modern Life* (Cambridge: Harvard Univ. Press, 1994). Kegan mentions religion only in passing (pp. 266ff.).

Chapter 2: Born into a Plural World

[1]For the following see, for example, the impressive bibliography compiled in the volume by Marcia J. Bunge, ed., *The Child in Christian Thought* (Grand Rapids: Eerdmans, 2001), 490–97 on "History of Childhood and Contemporary Issues Regarding Children."

[2]Neil Postman, *The Disappearance of Childhood* (New York: Delacorte, 1982).

[3]For a detailed description and for references to the sources, see Friedrich Schweitzer, *Die Religion des Kindes. Zur Problemgeschichte einer religionspädagogischen Grundfrage* (Gütersloh: Gütersloher Verlagshaus, 1992); see also the various historical chapters in Bunge, *The Child.*

[4]Schweitzer, *Die Religion des Kindes*, with detailed references.

[5]Johann Heinrich Pestalozzi, *Wie Gertrud ihre Kinder lehrt, ein Versuch, den Müttern Anleitung zu geben, ihre Kinder selbst zu unterrichten in Briefen von Heinrich Pestalozzi* (1801), Sämtliche Werke, vol. 13 (Berlin/Leipzig: 1927), 353.

[6]Friedrich Schleiermacher, *Erziehungslehre* (Berlin: G. Reimer, 1849), 659f.

[7]Jean-Jacques Rousseau, *Oeuvres Complètes*, vol. 4, *Émile* (Paris: Gallimard, 1969), 553ff.

[8]For a critical discussion (and references to Freud's writings), see Ana-Maria Rizzuto, *The Birth of the Living God: A Psychoanalytic Study* (Chicago: Univ. of Chicago Press, 1979), 13–53.

[9]Erik H. Erikson, *Childhood and Society,* 2d ed. (New York: Norton, 1963); idem, *Young Man Luther: A Study in Psychoanalysis and History* (New York: Norton, 1958); idem, *Insight and Responsibility* (New York: Norton, 1964); idem, *Life History and the Historical Moment* (New York: Norton, 1975); idem, *Gandhi's Truth: On the Origins of Militant Nonviolence* (New York: Norton, 1969); idem, *Identity: Youth and Crisis* (New York: Norton, 1968); idem, *Identity and the Life Cycle* (New York: International Universities Press, 1959); idem, *The Life Cycle Completed: A Review* (New York: Norton, 1982); and other books; see J. Eugene Wright, *Erikson: Identity and Religion* (New York: Seabury, 1982); Hetty Zock, *A Psychology of Ultimate Concern: Erik H. Erikson's Contribution to the Psychology of Religion* (Amsterdam and Atlanta: Rodopi, 1990).

[10]Erikson, *Young Man Luther,* 118.

[11]Quoted according to Karl Ernst Nipkow, *Bildung in einer pluralen Welt. Vol. 2: Religionspädagogik im Pluralismus* (Gütersloh: Kaiser/Gütersloher Verlagshaus, 1998), 145f.

[12]Martha Fay, *Do Children Need Religion? How Parents Today Are Thinking about the Big Questions* (New York: Pantheon, 1993), 202.

[13]A general statement is offered by Alice Miller, *For Your Own Good: Hidden Cruelty in Child-Rearing and the Roots of Violence* (New York: Noonday, 1983). See also Philipp Greven, *Spare the Child: The Religious Roots of Punishment and the Psychological Impact of Physical Abuse* (New York: Knopf, 1991); Donald Capps, *The Child's Song: The Religious Abuse of Children* (Louisville: Westminster John Knox Press, 1995). For a discussion, see Bunge, *The Child,* "Introduction," 5. From the German literature, see Dagmar Scherf, ed., *Der liebe Gott sieht alles. Erfahrungen mit religiöser Sozialisation* (Frankfurt am Main: Fischer, 1984); Jutta Richter, *Himmel, Hölle, Fegefeuer. Versuch einer Befreiung* (Reinbek: Rowohlt, 1985); Karl Frielingsdorf, *Dämonische Gottesbilder. Ihre Entstehung, Entlarvung und Überwindung* (Mainz: M. Grünewald, 1992); Helmut Jaschke, *Dunkle Gottesbilder. Therapeutische Wege der Heilung* (Freiburg: Herder, 1992).

[14]Allen Wheelis, *The Quest for Identity* (New York: Norton, 1958), 51.

[15]Tilmann Moser, *Gottesvergiftung* (Frankfurt am Main: Suhrkamp, 1976).

[16]Monika Schaefer, *Weil ich beim Beten lügen mußte. Rekonstruktion einer verlorenen Kindheit* (Stuttgart: Kreuz, 1992), 51.

[17]I have not found a specific study on this view but similar arguments can be found in the general feminist literature on the role of the mother. See the now classic statement by Nancy Chodorow, *The Reproduction of Mothering: Psychoanalysis and the Sociology of Gender* (Berkeley: University of California Press, 1978).

[18]The family is itself considered a private realm. Consequently, little is known about the religious nurture or education taking place in the family. See Merton Strommen and Richard Hardel, *Passing on the Faith: A Radical New Model for Youth and Family Ministry* (Winona: St. Mary's Press, 2000); Michael E. Ebertz, "'Heilige Familie'– ein Auslaufmodell? Religiöse Kompetenz der Familien in soziologischer Sicht," in *Gottesbeziehung in der Familie. Familienkatechetische Orientierungen von der Kindertaufe bis ins Jugendalter,* ed. Albert Biesinger and Herbert Bendel (Ostfildern: Schwaben, 2000), 16–43; as a general background, Don Browning et al., *From Culture Wars to Common Ground: Religion and the American Family Debate* (Louisville: Westminster John Knox Press, 1997).

[19]For empirical data on the religious orientations of today's parents, see the studies by Wade Clark Roof, *A Generation of Seekers: The Spiritual Journeys of the Baby Boom Generation* (San Francisco: Harper & Row, 1993); idem, *Spiritual Marketplace: Baby Boomers and the Remaking of American Religion* (Princeton: Princeton Univ. Press, 1999).

[20]See note 13.

[21]Douglas Coupland, *Life after God* (London: Touchstone, 1995), 178 and 161.

[22]In 1995, Lorie A'lise Sousa, "Interfaith Marriage and the Individual and Family Life Cycle," *Family Therapy* 22 (1995): 97–104; p. 97 mentions 375,000 interfaith couples in the United States. The majority of them combine a Jewish and a Christian background.

[23]In a interview in *The New York Times Magazine* in May 1988, Harvey Cox says: "we're in a stage now in the relationship between Jewish and Christians in which a child can grow up being part of both these traditions without violating either one. He'll be raised Jewish and he'll get the 'Christian Addendum' to the Jewish Story," quoted according to Fay, *Do Children Need Religion?*, 198.

[24]Fay, *Do Children Need Religion?*, 196.

[25]See, for example, the publications by authors such as John Hicks or Paul Knitter.

[26]Regine Froese, "'Für mich sind Muslime und Christen dasselbe...' Junge Erwachsene aus christlich-muslimischen Familien," *Zeitschrift für Pädagogik und Theologie* 52 (2000): 171–86.

[27]For a good review of the most important trends affecting families, see Don S. Browning et al., *Culture Wars to Common Ground*, 51–72; see also Solly Dreman, ed., *The Family on the Threshold of the 21st Century: Trends and Implications* (Mahwah, N. J.: L. Erlbaum, 1997); William C. Nichols and Mary Anne Pace-Nichols, eds., *Handbook of Family Development and Intervention* (New York: J. Wiley, 2000).

[28]This is the strength–and the weakness–of much of the literature from the United Kingdom: for example, John Hull, *Studies in Religion and Education* (London: Falmer Press, 1984); Robert Jackson, *Religious Education: An Interpretive Approach* (London: Hodder & Stoughton, 1997). For the American discussion, see Norma H. Thompson, ed., *Religious Pluralism and Religious Education* (Birmingham, Ala.: Religious Education Press, 1988); Barbara Wilkerson, ed., *Multicultural Religious Education* (Birmingham, Ala.: Religious Education Press, 1997).

[29]Coupland, *Life after God*, 5f.

[30]Friedrich Schweitzer, *Das Recht des Kindes auf Religion. Ermutigungen für Eltern und Erzieher* (Gütersloh: Gütersloher Verlagshaus, 2000).

[31]See Bunge, *The Child.*

Chapter 3: In Search of a Faith of One's Own

[1]*Growing Up Postmodern: Imitating Christ in the Age of "Whatever,"* The 1998 Princeton Lectures on Youth, Church, and Culture (Princeton, N.J.: Princeton Theological Seminary, 1999).

[2]See Friedrich Schweitzer, *Die Suche nach eigenem Glauben. Einführung in die Religionspädagogik des Jugendalters* (Gütersloh: Gütersloher Verlagshaus, 1996).

[3]John Westerhoff, *Will Our Children Have Faith?* (New York: Seabury Press, 1976).

[4]The essays mentioned in note 1 are a good example.

[5]See Philippe Ariès, *Centuries of Childhood: A Social History of Family Life* (New York: Vintage, 1962), 29: "People had no idea of what we call adolescence, and the idea was a long time taking shape," referring to the time before the eighteenth century; see also Joseph F. Kett, *Rites of Passage: Adolescence in America 1790 to the Present* (New York: Basic Books, 1977); for the European experience, John R. Gillis, *Youth and History: Tradition and Change in European Age Relations 1770–Present* (New York: Academic Press, 1974).

[6]The classical study comes from Arnold van Gennep, *Les rites de passage: Étude systématique des rites (1909)* (Paris: É. Nourry, 1981); for current views, see Gunther Klosinski, ed., *Pubertätsriten. Äquivalente und Defizite in unserer Gesellschaft* (Bern: Huber, 1991).

[7]Van Gennep, *Les rites*, offers vivid accounts of some of these rites.

[8]Ariès, *Centuries of Childhood;* Kett, *Rites;* also Michael Mitterauer, *Sozialgeschichte der Jugend* (Frankfurt am Main: Suhrkamp, 1986).

[9]Jean-Jacques Rousseau, *Oeuvres Complètes,* vol. 4,: *Émile* (Paris: Gallimard, 1969). Book 4 is devoted to adolescence.

[10]G. Stanley Hall, *Adolescence, Its Psychology and Its Relations to Physiology, Anthropology, Sociology, Sex Crime, Religion and Education* (New York: D. Appleton, 1905).
[11]Erik H. Erikson, *Identity, Youth, and Crisis* (New York: Norton, 1968); idem, *Young Man Luther: A Study in Psychoanalysis and History* (New York: Norton, 1958). His earlier publications had already paved the way; see idem, *Childhood and Society* (New York: Norton, 1950) with important passages on identity in adolescence.
[12]James Joyce, *A Portrait of the Artist as a Young Man* (New York: Viking Press, 1916); Hermann Hesse, *Demian: The Story of Emil Sinclair's Youth* (New York: Harper & Row, 1965). For a collection on the 1960s' discussion, see Erik H. Erikson, ed., *Youth: Change and Challenge* (New York: Basic Books, 1963).
[13]See Don S. Browning, *Generative Man: Psychoanalytic Perspectives* (New York: Delta, 1975).
[14]A good example from his extensive work is Talcott Parsons, "Youth in the Context of American Society," in *The Challenge of Youth*, ed. Erik H. Erikson (Garden City: Doubleday, 1965), 110-41.
[15]See especially Mitterauer, *Sozialgeschichte;* Kett, *Rites;* also Gillis, *Youth and History.*
[16]On the history of confirmation, see Richard R. Osmer, *Confirmation: Presbyterian Practices in Ecumenical Perspective* (Louisville: Geneva Press, 1996).
[17]Most notably Kett, *Rites.*
[18]See among others, Hans Küng, *Does God Exist? An Answer For Today* (Garden City: Doubleday, 1980); Wolfhart Pannenberg, *Anthropology in Theological Perspective* (Philadelphia: Westminster Press, 1985); Donald Capps, *Pastoral Care: A Thematic Approach* (Philadelphia: Westminster Press, 1979); Hans Jürgen Fraas, *Glaube und Identität. Grundlegung einer Didaktik religiöser Lernprozesse* (Göttingen: Vandenhoeck & Ruprecht, 1983); Friedrich Schweitzer, *Lebensgeschichte und Religion. Religiöse Entwicklung und Erziehung im Kindes- und Jugendalter* (Munich: Kaiser, 1987).
[19]Erikson, *Young Man Luther*, 41–43, 118f.
[20]See for further background, Erik H. Erikson, *Life History and the Historical Moment* (New York: Norton, 1975).
[21]Erikson, *Young Man Luther*, 118.
[22]Erikson, *Identity*, 38.
[23]Erickson, *Identity*, 30–38.
[24]See Kenneth J. Gergen, *Saturated Self: Dilemmas of Identity in Contemporary Life* (New York: Basic Books, 1991); Heiner Keupp and Renate Höfer, eds., *Identitätsarbeit heute. Klassische und aktuelle Perspektiven der Identitätsforschung* (Frankfurt am Main.: Suhrkamp, 1997); Heiner Keupp, ed., *Zugänge zum Subjekt. Perspektiven einer reflexiven Sozialpsychologie* (Frankfurt am Main: Suhrkamp, 1994); Anthony Giddens, *Modernity and Self-Identity: Self and Society in the Late Modern Age* (Stanford: Stanford Univ. Press, 1991). For additional aspects, see also Scott Bukatman, *Terminal Identity: The Virtual Subject in Postmodern Science Fiction* (Durham, N.C.: Duke Univ. Press, 1993); Jonathan S. Epstein, ed., *Youth Culture: Identity in a Postmodern World* (Malden and Oxford: Blackwell, 1998).
[25]This critique is in part also present in the literature mentioned in note 24. The most important challenge from the perspective of gender has come from Carol Gilligan, *In a Different Voice: Psychological Theory and Women's Development* (Cambridge: Harvard Univ: Press, 1982); see also Mary Field Belenky et al., *Women's Ways of Knowing: The Development of Self, Voice and Mind* (New York: Basic Books, 1986).
[26]I have discussed such changes at length in Schweitzer, *Die Suche.*
[27]Deutsche Shell, ed., *Jugend 2000*, vol. 1 (Opladen: Leske & Budrich, 2000).
[28]See from a sociological perspective, Wade Clark Roof, "At-Risk Youth," in *At-Risk Youth, At-Risk Church: What Jesus Christ and American Teenagers Are Saying to the Mainline Church, The 1997 Princeton Lectures on Youth, Church, and Culture* (Princeton: Institute for Youth Ministry, 1998), 86.
[29]Gergen, *Saturated Self;* Keupp, *Zugänge zum Subjekt.*
[30]Gilligan, *Different Voice.*
[31]Gilligan, *Different Voice*, 11–13.

[32]Gilligan, *Different Voice*, esp. 151–74.

[33]The image of "patchwork identities" is found especially in the work of Keupp, *Zugänge zum Subjekt.*

[34]See Wade Clark Roof et al., eds., *The Post-War Generation and Establishment Religion: Cross-Cultural Perspectives* (Boulder, Colo.: Westview Press, 1995); Ulrich Nembach, ed., *Jugend–2000 Jahre nach Jesus. Jugend und Religion in Europa II. Bericht vom 2. Internationalen Göttinger Religionssoziologischen Symposion* (Frankfurt am Main: P. Lang, 1996); Roland J. Campiche, ed., *Cultures jeunes et religions en Europe* (Paris: Éd. du Cerf, 1997).

[35]Thomas Luckmann, "Bemerkungen zu Gesellschaftsstruktur, Bewußtseinsformen und Religion in der modernen Gesellschaft, in *Soziologie und gesellschaftliche Entwicklung. Verhandlungen des 22. Deutschen Soziologentages in Dortmund 1984*, ed. Burkard Lutz (Frankfurt am Main: Campus, 1985), 475–84.

[36]This is the main conclusion of my analysis in Schweitzer, *Die Suche.*

[37]This is also discussed, from a different perspective, by Richard Osmer, *A Teachable Spirit: Recovering the Teaching Office in the Church* (Louisville: Westminster/John Knox, 1990).

[38]See Nembach, *Jugend*; see also the Swiss study: Alfred Dubach and Roland J. Campiche, eds., *Jede(r) ein Sonderfall? Religion in der Schweiz. Ergebnisse einer Repräsentativbefragung* (Zürich: NZN, 1993).

[39]Peter König, "Wir Vodookinder," in *Deutsche Jugend. Kursbuch 113*, ed. Karl Markus Michel and Tilman Spengler (Berlin: Berlin-Verlag, 1993), 1–6.

[40]For a summary of the pertinent literature, see Schweitzer, *Die Suche.*

[41]See Karl Ernst Nipkow, *Erwachsenwerden ohne Gott? Gotteserfahrung im Lebenslauf* (Munich: Kaiser, 1987); Günther Leyh, *Mit der Jugend von Gott sprechen. Gottesbilder kirchlich orientierter Jugendlicher im Horizont korrelativer Theologie* (Stuttgart: Kohlhammer, 1994).

[42]Reported by Leyh, *Mit der Jugend*, 42.

[43]James W. Fowler, *Stages of Faith: The Psychology of Human Development and the Quest for Meaning* (San Francisco: Harper & Row, 1981); for discussion, see James W. Fowler, Karl Ernst Nipkow, and Friedrich Schweitzer, eds., *Stages of Faith and Religious Development: Implications for Church, Education, and Society* (New York: Crossroad, 1991).

[44]It should be clearly mentioned that Fowler's later work points exactly in this directions; see his *Weaving the New Creation: Stages of Faith and the Public Church* (San Francisco: Harper & Row, 1991); idem, *Faithful Change: The Personal and Public Challenges of Postmodern Life* (Nashville: Abingdon, 1996).

[45]Especially by Robert Kegan, *In Over Our Heads: The Mental Demands of Modern Life* (Cambridge: Harvard Univ. Press, 1994).

[46]For references concerning postadolescence, see chapter 4.

[47]A vivid example from Germany is Heiner Barz, *Postmoderne Religion am Beispiel der jungen Generation in den Alten Bundesländern* (Opladen: Leske & Budrich, 1992).

[48]See Osmer, *Confirmation*; William R. Meyers, ed., *Becoming and Belonging: A Practical Design for Confirmation* (Cleveland: United Church Press, 1993); Schweitzer, *Die Suche*, 179–95.

[49]For a classic statement that is still worth reading, see Peter Blos, *On Adolescence: A Psychoanalytic Interpretation* (New York: Macmillan, 1962).

[50]Lyn Mikel Brown and Carol Gilligan, *Meeting at the Crossroads: Women's Psychology and Girls' Development* (New York: Ballantine, 1992).

[51]See the several studies by Wade Clark Roof, especially *A Generation of Seekers: The Spiritual Journeys of the Baby Boom Generation* (San Francisco: HarperSan Francisco, 1993).

[52]David Tracy, *Blessed Rage for Order: The New Pluralism in Theology*, 2d ed. (Chicago: Univ. of Chicago Press, 1996).

[53]To just mention two examples from the field of practical theology and religious education: Don S. Browning, *A Fundamental Practical Theology: Descriptive and Strategic Proposals* (Minneapolis: Fortress Press, 1991); Georg Baudler, *Korrelationsdidaktik: Leben*

durch Glauben erschließen. Theorie und Praxis der Korrelation von Glaubensüberlieferung und Lebenserfahrung auf der Grundlage von Symbolen und Sakramenten (Paderborn: F. Schöningh, 1984).

[54]The study has not yet been published. It was part of larger study on globalization and religion, sponsored by the Institute for Youth Ministry, Princeton Theological Seminary.

[55]See, for example, T. Beaudoin, *Virtual Faith: The Irreverent Spiritual Quest of Generation X* (San Francisco: Jossey-Bass, 1998); for the German literature, see Friedrich Schweitzer, "Jugendkultur und Religionspädagogik," in *Religionspädagogik und Kultur. Beiträge zu einer religionspädagogischen Theorie kulturell vermittelter Praxis in Kirche und Gesellschaft,* ed. Peter Biehl and Klaus Wegenast (Neukirchen/Vluyn: Neukirchener Verlag, 2000), 165–78.

[56]A. Gödicke, "Evangelikalismus und Bekehrung. Qualitative Interviews mit Jugendlichen in der Schweiz," in *Fundamentalistische Jugendkultur,* ed. Bernhard Dressler et al. (Loccum: Religionspädagogisches Institut, 1995), 114–31. For general background, see Martin E. Marty and R. Scott Appleby, eds., *The Fundamentalism Project,* 5 vols. (Chicago: Univ. of Chicago Press, 1991–1995); Friedrich Schweitzer, "Fundamentalismus– Chance oder Risiko der religiösen Entwicklung?" in *Christlicher Wahrheitsanspruch zwischen Fundamentalismus und Pluralität,* ed. Ulrich Kühn et al. (Leipzig: Evangelische Verlagsanstalt, 1998), 41–58.

[57]For an introduction that is still helpful, see Gerhad Ebeling, *Luther. Einführung in sein Denken* (Tübingen: Mohr [P. Siebeck], 1964).

[58]Wolfhart Pannenberg, *Anthropology in Theological Perspective* (Philadelphia: Westminster Press, 1985), gives a detailed account of this understanding.

[59]Henning Luther, *Religion und Alltag. Bausteine zu einer Praktischen Theologie des Subjekts* (Stuttgart: Radius, 1992), 160–83.

[60]Michael Welker, *Gottes Gist. Theologie des Heiligen Geistes* (Neukirchen-Vluyn: Neukirchener Verlag, 1992), 32–37.

Chapter 4: Religious Affiliation and Distancing in Postadolescence

[1]One of the first researchers to speak of "postadolescence" and of "postmodern" youth was Kenneth Keniston, *Young Radicals: Notes on Committed Youth* (New York: Harcourt, Brace & World, 1968), esp. 257–90.

[2]Klaus Engelhardt et al., eds., *Fremde Heimat Kirche. Die dritte EKD-Erhebung über Kirchenmitgliedschaft* (Gütersloh: Gütersloher Verlagshaus, 1997), 311.

[3]For example, Armin Kuphal, *Abschied von der Kirche* (Gelnhausen: Burckhardthaus, 1979), 77; Ulrich Müller-Weißner and Rainer Volz, "Kirchenaustritte aus der Evangelischen Kirche," in *Kirche ohne Volk. Kirchenaustritte. Interpretationen und Schlußfolgerungen,* ed. Ulrich Müller-Weißner et al. (Speyer: Evangelischer Presseverlag Pfalz, 1991), 19.

[4]Wade Clark Roof and William McKinney, *American Mainline Religion: Its Changing Shape and Future* (New Brunswick, N.J.: Rutgers Univ. Press, 1987), 181.

[5]Schweizerisches Pastoralsoziologisches Institut, ed., *Jenseits der Kirchen–Analyse und Auseinandersetzung mit einem neuen Phänomen in unserer Gesellschaft* (Zürich: NZN, 1998), 41.

[6]Andreas Feige, "Kirche auf dem Prüfstand: Die Radikalität der 18-20 jährigen. Biographische und epochale Elemente im Verhältnis der Jugend zur Kirche–ein Vergleich zwischen 1972 und 1982," in *Kirchenmitgliedschaft im Wandel. Untersuchungen zur Realität der Volkskirche. Beiträge zur zweiten EKD-Umfrage "Was wird aus der Kirche?"* ed. Joachim Matthes (Gütersloh: Gütersloher Verlagshaus, 1990), 65–98; Engelhardt et al., *Fremde Heimat Kirche,* 89ff.; Joachim Eiben, "Kirche und Religion–Säkularisierung als sozialistisches Erbe?" in *Jugend '92. vol. 2: Im Spiegel der Wissenschaften,* ed. Jugendwerk der Deutschen Shell (Opladen: Leske & Budrich, 1992), 91–104; for an overview, see Friedrich Schweitzer, *Die Suche nach eigenem Glauben. Einführung in die Religionspädagogik des Jugendalters* (Gütersloh: Gütersloher Verlagshaus, 1996).

[7]See Jürgen Henkys and Friedrich Schweitzer, "Atheism, Religion, and Indifference in the Two Parts of Germany: Before and After 1989," in *Leaving Religion and Religious Life*, ed. Mordechai Bar-Lev and William Shaffir (Greenwich: JAI, 1997), 117–38.

[8]See Engelhardt et al., *Fremde Heimat Kirche*, 315; Gert Pickel, "Dimensionen religiöser Überzeugungen bei jungen Erwachsenen in den Neuen und Alten Bundesländern der Bundesrepublik Deutschland," *Kölner Zeitschrift für Soziologie und Sozialpsychologie 47* (1995): 516–34.

[9]Mordechai Bar-Lev et al., "Culture-specific Factors Which Cause Jews in Israel to Abandon Religious Practice," in *Leaving Religion and Religious Life*, ed. Mordechai Bar-Lev and William Shaffir (Greenwich: JAI, 1997), 185–204.

[10]For an especially clear example, see Gerhard Schmidtchen, *Was den Deutschen heilig ist. Religiöse und politische Strömungen in der Bundesrepublik Deutschland* (Munich: Kösel, 1979), 28.

[11]See Eiben, "Kirche und Religion"; Gerhard Schmidtchen, *Ethik und Protest. Moralbilder und Wertkonflikte junger Menschen* (Opladen: Leske & Budrich, 1993).

[12]Erik H. Erikson, *Young Man Luther: A Study in Psychoanalysis and History* (New York: Norton, 1958), 102–4.

[13]For a discussion, see Feige, "Kirche auf dem Prüfstand."

[14]Lawrence Kohlberg, *The Psychology of Moral Development: The Nature and Validity of Moral Stages* (San Francisco: Harper & Row, 1984).

[15]Among others, see William G. Perry, *Forms of Intellectual and Ethical Development in the College Years: A Scheme* (New York: Holt, Rinehart & Winston, 1968); James W. Fowler, *Stages of Faith: The Psychology of Human Development and the Quest for Meaning* (San Francisco: Harper & Row, 1981); Fritz Oser and Paul Gmünder, *Der Mensch–Stufen seiner religiösen Entwicklung. Ein strukturgenetischer Ansatz* (Zürich: Benziger, 1984).

[16]Robert Schuster, ed., *Was sie glauben. Texte von Jugendlichen* (Stuttgart: Steinkopff, 1984), 251.

[17]Fowler, *Stages of Faith*, 184–98, with reference to Paul Ricoeur.

[18]Robert Wuthnow, *The Restructuring of American Religion: Society and Faith Since World War II* (Princeton: Princeton Univ. Press, 1988); Rüdiger Schloz, "Das Bildungsdilemma der Kirche," in *Kirchenmitgliedschaft im Wandel. Untersuchungen zur Realität der Volkskirche. Beiträge zur zweiten EKD-Umfrage "Was wird aus der Kirche?"* ed. Joachim Matthes (Gütersloh: Gütersloher Verlagshaus, 1990), 215–30.

[19]Oser and Gmünder, *Der Mensch*, 201.

[20]Evangelische Kirche in Deutschland, *Der Dienst der evangelischen Kirche an der Hochschule. Eine Studie im Auftrag der Synode der EKD* (Gütersloh: Gütersloher Verlagshaus, 1991).

[21]See Engelhardt et al., *Fremde Heimat Kirche*; Roof and McKinney, *American Mainline Religion*.

[22]Wuthnow, *Restructuring of American Religion;* Karl Gabriel, *Christentum zwischen Tradition und Postmoderne* (Freiburg: Herder, 1993); Wade Clark Roof et al., eds., *The Post-War Generation and Establishment Religion: Cross-Cultural Perspectives* (Boulder, Colo.: Westview Press, 1995).

[23]Wade Clark Roof, *A Generation of Seekers: The Spiritual Journeys of the Baby Boom Generation* (San Francisco: Harper & Row, 1993).

[24]Ulrich Schwab, *Familienreligiosität. Religiöse Traditionen im Prozeß der Generationen* (Stuttgart: Kohlhammer, 1995).

[25]Jürgen Zinnecker and Rainer K. Silbereisen, *Kindheit in Deutschland. Aktueller Survey über Kinder und ihre Eltern* (Weinheim: Juventa, 1996).

[26]See Pickel, "Dimensionen religiöser Überzeugungen," 526; Henkys and Schweitzer, "Atheism, Religion and Indifference."

[27]Erik H. Erikson, *Identity, Youth, and Crisis* (New York: Norton, 1968); Daniel J. Levinson, *The Seasons of a Man's Life* (New York: Ballantine, 1978); Carol Gilligan, *In a Different Voice* (Cambridge: Harvard Univ. Press, 1982); for a helpful discussion, see Robert C. Aylmer, "The Launching of the Single Young Adult," in *The Changing Family*

Life Cycle: A Framework for Family Therapy, ed. Betty Carter and Monica McGoldrick, 2d ed. (Boston: Allyn & Bacon, 1989), 191–208.

²⁸Kenniston, *Young Radicals.*

²⁹Fowler, *Stages of Faith;* idem, *Becoming Adult Becoming Christian: Adult Development and Christian Faith* (San Francisco: Harper & Row, 1984); idem, *Faith Development and Pastoral Care* (Philadelphia: Fortress Press, 1987), 68–71.

³⁰Evelyn Eaton Whitehead and James D. Whitehead, *Christian Life Patterns: The Psychological Challenges and Religious Invitations of Adult Life* (Garden City: Image, 1979), 63–118.

³¹Sharon Parks, *The Critical Years: The Young Adult Search for a Faith to Live By* (San Francisco: Harper & Row, 1986), xii.

³²See Parks, *Critical Years,* 133–76.

³³For a good beginning, see Harley Atkinson, ed., *Handbook of Young Adult Religious Education* (Birmingham: Religious Education Press, 1995); see also Norbert Copray, *Jung und trotzdem erwachsen,* 2 vols. (Düsseldorf: 1987–1988).

³⁴Aylmer, "Launching"; Whitehead and Whitehead, *Christian Life Patterns.*

³⁵V. Bailey Gillespie, *The Experience of Faith* (Birmingham: Religious Education Press, 1988), 175–92, speaks of "Reordered Faith" in this context; see also Parks, *Critical Years.*

Chapter 5: Church, Individual Religion, Public Responsibility

¹Immanuel Kant, "Beantwortung der Frage: 'Was ist Aufklärung?'" in *Werke,* vol. 4 (Frankfurt am Main: Insel, 1964), 51–61. The famous opening passage is: "*Aufklärung ist der Ausgang des Menschen aus seiner selbst verschuldeten Unmündigkeit. Unmündigkeit* ist das Unvermögen, sich seines Verstandes ohne Leitung eines anderen zu bedienen. *Selbstverschuldet* ist diese Unmündigkeit, wenn die Ursache derselben nicht am Mangel des Verstandes, sondern der Entschließung und des Mutes liegt, sich seiner ohne Leitung eines andern zu bedienen. Sapere aude! Habe Mut dich deines *eigenen* Verstandes zu bedienen! ist also der Wahlspruch der Aufklärung."

²See the discussions in Neil J. Smelser and Erik H. Erikson, eds., *Themes of Work and Love in Adulthood* (Cambridge: Harvard University Press, 1980).

³See Erik H. Erikson, *Childhood and Society* (New York: Norton, 1950, 1963); idem, *Identity, Youth, and Crisis* (New York: Norton, 1968); idem, *Insight and Responsibility* (New York: Norton, 1964); also see the chapters on Erikson in my books: Friedrich Schweitzer, *Identität und Religion. Religiöse Entwicklung und Erziehung im Kindes- und Jugendalter* (Munich: Kaiser, 1987).

⁴Erik H. Erikson, "On the Generational Cycle: An Address," in *International Journal of Psychoanalysis* 61 (1980): 213–23.

⁵Most clearly in Erik H. Erikson, *Young Man Luther: A Study in Psychoanalysis and History* (New York: Norton, 1958).

⁶Dietrich Rössler, *Grundriß der Praktischen Theologie* (Berlin: de Gruyter, 1986).

⁷Daniel J. Levinson, *The Seasons of a Man's Life* (New York: Ballantine, 1978); idem, *The Seasons of a Woman's Life* (New York: Knopf, 1996).

⁸Levinson, *Man's Life,* 57.

⁹Wade Clark Roof, "At-Risk Youth," in *At-Risk Youth, At-Risk Church: What Jesus Christ and American Teenagers Are Saying to the Mainline Church. The 1997 Princeton Lectures on Youth, Church, and Culture* (Princeton: Institute for Youth Ministry, 1998), 86.

¹⁰Don S. Browning et al., *From Culture Wars to Common Ground: Religion and the American Family Debate* (Louisville: Westminister John Knox Press, 1997), 52.

¹¹For Germany for example, see Rosemarie Nave-Herz, *Familie heute: Wandel der Familienstrukturen und Folgen für die Erziehung* (Darmstadt: Wissenschaftliche Buchgesellschaft, 199); Deutscher Bundestag, ed., *Zehnter Kinder- und Jugendbericht vom 25.8.1998* (Bonn: Deutscher Bundestag, 1998).

¹²Elisabeth Beck-Gernsheim, *Was kommt nach der Familie? Einblicke in neue Lebensformen* (Munich: Beck, 1998).

[13]Neil Postman, *The Disappearance of Childhood* (New York: Delacorte, 1982).
[14]As mentioned in chapter 1, the work of Harvey Cox is especially indicative of such developments.
[15]For my own views, see Wolfgang Lück and Friedrich Schweitzer, *Religiöse Bildung Erwachsener. Grundlagen und Impulse für die Praxis* (Stuttgart: W. Kohlhammer, 1999).
[16]Wade Clark Roof and William McKinney, *American Mainline Religion: Its Changing Shape and Future* (New Brunswick, N.J.: Rutgers Univ. Press, 1987).
[17]Alfred Dubach and Roland J. Campiche, eds., *Jede(r) ein Sonderfall? Religion in der Schweiz. Ergebnisse einer Repräsentativbefragung* (Zürich: NZN-Buchverlag, F. Reinhardt, 1993).
[18]For additional references, see Lück and Schweitzer, *Religiöse Bildung Erwachsener.*
[19]Cf. José Casanova, *Public Religions in the Modern World* (Chicago: Univ. of Chicago Press, 1994); Peter Beyer, *Religion und Globalization* (London: Sage, 1994).
[20]From this discussion, see Parker J. Palmer, *The Company of Strangers: Christians and the Renewal of America's Public Life* (New York: Crossroad, 1981); Jean L. Cohen and Andrew Arato, *Civil Society and Political Theory* (London: Cambridge Univ. Press, 1992); Michael Walzer, ed., *Toward a Global Civil Society* (Providence: Berghahn, 1995).
[21]Robert Wuthnow, *Christianity and Civil Society: The Contemporary Debate* (Valley Forge, Pa.: Trinity Press, 1996).
[22]See, for example, the discussions in Friedrich Schweitzer and Johannes van der Ven, eds., *Practical Theology—International Perspectives* (Frankfurt am Main: P. Lang, 1999); Marcel Viau, James Poling, and Friedrich Schweitzer, "Perspectives on Practical Theologies and Methodologies," in *Globalization and Difference: Practical Theology in a World Context,* ed. Paul Ballard and Pamela Couture (Cardiff: Academic Press, 1999), 193–212.
[23]Paul Ricoeur, *The Symbolism of Evil* (Boston: Beacon Press, 1967).
[24]Friedrich Schleiermacher, *Die Weihnachtsfeier. Ein Gespräch* (Halle: Schimmelpfennig, 1806).
[25]Henning Luther, *Religion und Alltag. Bausteine zu einer Praktischen Theologie des Subjekts* (Stuttgart: Radius, 1992), 160–83.
[26]Carol Gilligan, *In a Different Voice: Psychological Theory and Women's Development* (Cambridge: Harvard Univ. Press, 1982); Mary Field Belenky et al., *Women's Ways of Knowing: The Development of Self, Voice, and Mind* (New York: Basic Books, 1986).
[27]See the major accounts: Wolfhart Pannenberg, *Anthropology in Theological Perspective* (Philadelphia: Westminster Press, 1985); Hans Walter Wolff, *Anthropologie des Alten Testaments* (Munich: Kaiser, 1973).
[28]Browning et al., *Culture Wars.*
[29]Browning et al., *Culture Wars,* 1.
[30]See Alasdair MacIntyre, *After Virtue: A Study in Moral Theory* (Notre Dame: Univ. of Notre Dame Press, 1981); Stanley Hauerwas, *A Community of Character: Toward a Constructive Christian Social Ethic* (Notre Dame: Notre Dame Univ. Press, 1981). For a helpful introduction, see Micha Brumlik and Hauke Brunkhorst, eds., *Gemeinschaft und Gerechtigkeit* (Frankfurt am Main: Fischer, 1993).
[31]Jürgen Habermas, *The Theory of Communication Action,* 2 vols. (Boston: Beacon Press, 1984, 1987). For a theological discussion, see Don S. Browning and Francis Schüssler Fiorenza, eds., *Habermas, Modernity, and Public Theology* (New York: Crossroad, 1992).
[32]For theological discussions and visions of the church, see Jürgen Moltmann, *The Church in the Power of the Spirit: A Contribution of Messianic Ecclesiology* (London: SCM Press, 1977); Eilert Herms, *Kirche für die Welt. Lage und Aufgabe der evangelischen Kirche im vereinigten Deutschland* (Tübingen: Mohr, 1995); Michael Welker, *Kirche im Pluralismus* (Gütersloh: Gütersloher Verlagshaus, 1995); Wolfgang Huber, *Kirche in der Zeitenwende. Gesellschaftlicher Wandel und Erneuerung der Kirche* (Gütersloh: Bertelsmann Stiftung, 1998).
[33]See James W. Fowler, *Weaving the New Creation: Stages of Faith and the Public Church* (San Francisco: Harper 1991); idem, *Faithful Change: The Personal and Public*

Challenges of Postmodern Life (Nashville: Abingdon Press, 1996); see also Jack L. Seymour et al., *The Church in the Education of the Public: Refocusing the Task of Religious Education* (Nashville: Abingdon Press, 1984).

Chapter 6: Between Adulthood and Old Age

[1]Erik H. Erikson must be honored for one the earliest ventures into this field of adult developmental psychology; see his *Childhood and Society*, 1st ed. (New York: Norton, 1950), esp. the seminal chapter on the "Eight Ages of Man."

[2]One of the clearest examples still is James W. Fowler, *Stages of Faith: The Psychology of Human Development and the Quest for Meaning* (San Francisco: Harper & Row, 1981).

[3]See my books: Friedrich Schweitzer, *Lebensgeschichte und Religion. Religiöse Entwicklung und Erziehung im Kindes- und Jugendalter* (Munich: Kaiser, 1987); idem, *Die Religion des Kindes. Zur Problemgeschichte einer religionspädagogischen Grundfrage* (Gütersloh: Gütersloher Verlagshaus, 1992); idem, *Die Suche nach eigenem Glauben. Einführung in die Religionspädagogik des Jugendalters* (Gütersloh: Gütersloher Verlagshaus, 1996); Wolfgang Lück and Friedrich Schweitzer, *Religiöse Bildung Erwachsener. Grundlagen und Impulse für die Praxis* (Stuttgart: Kohlhammer, 1999).

[4]Peter Laslett, *A Fresh Map of Life: The Emergence of the Third Age* (London: Weidenfeld & Nicolson, 1989).

[5]See the discussions in Martina Blasberg-Kuhnke, *Gerontologie und Praktische Theologie. Studien zu einer Neuorientierung der Altenpastoral an der psychischen und gesellschaftlichen Wirklichkeit des alten Menschen* (Düsseldorf: Patmos, 1985); K. Brynolf Lyon, *Toward a Practical Theology of Aging* (Philadelphia: Fortress Press, 1985); Melvin A. Kimble et al., eds., *Aging, Spirituality, and Religion: A Handbook* (Minneapolis: Fortress Press, 1995).

[6]This concern is as widespread in the political discussions as in the academic literature; for a recent statement, see Beverly Goldberg, *Age Works: What Corporate America Must Do to Survive the Graying of the Workforce* (New York: The Free Press, 2000).

[7]For a summary, see Laslett, *Fresh Map*; Paul Johnson and Pat Thane, eds., *Old Age from Antiquity to Post-Modernity* (London: Routledge, 1998).

[8]Erik H. Erikson, *Childhood and Society*, 2d ed. (New York: Norton, 1963), 268.

[9]Ibid.

[10]See Johnson and Thane, *Old Age*; Peter Borscheid, "Der alte Mensch in der Vergangenheit," in *Alter und Altern: Ein interdisziplinärer Studientext zur Gerontologie*, ed. Paul B. Baltes et al. (Berlin: de Gruyter, 1994), 35–61.

[11]See Gerald J. Gruman, "Cultural Origins of Present-Day 'Age-ism': The Modernization of the Life Cycle," in *Aging and the Elderly: Humanistic Perspectives in Gerontology*, ed. Stuart F. Spicker et al. (Atlantic Highlands: Humanities Press, 1978), 359–87.

[12]See Laslett, *Fresh Map*; Baltes et al., *Alter und Altern;* Johnson and Thane, *Old Age*.

[13]Goldberg, *Age Works*.

[14]See Laslett, *Fresh Map*, 65.

[15]Erikson, *Childhood and Society*, 2d ed., 268.

[16]Erik H. Erikson, *Identity, Youth, and Crisis* (New York: Norton, 1968), 140.

[17]Erikson, *Identity*, 141.

[18]See Wade Clark Roof and William McKinney, *American Mainline Religion: Its Changing Shape and Future* (New Brunswick, N.J.: Rutgers Univ. Press, 1987); for examples from Germany, see Joachim Matthes, ed., *Kirchenmitgliedschaft im Wandel: Untersuchungen zur Realität der Volkskirche. Beiträge zur zweiten EKD-Umfrage "Was wird aus der Kirche?"* (Gütersloh: Gütersloher Verlagshaus, 1990).

[19]See Blasberg-Kuhnke, *Gerontologie und Praktische Theologie;* Lyon, *Practical Theology of Aging*.

[20]See the discussion by Blasberg-Kuhnke, *Gerontologie und Praktische Theologie*.

[21]For a good overview, see Deutsches Jugendinstitut, ed., *Wie geht's der Familie? Ein Handbuch zur Situation der Familien heute* (Munich: Kösel, 1988).

[22]Laslett, *Fresh Map*, 4.

[23]See Karl Ulrich Mayer and Paul B. Baltes, eds., *Die Berliner Altersstudie* (Berlin: Akademie Verlag, 1999); see also Baltes and Mittelstraß, op. cit.

[24]See the overviews in the following: Kimble et al., eds., *Aging, Spirituality, and Religion*; Harold G. Koenig, *Aging and God: Spiritual Pathways to Mental Health in Midlife and Later Years* (New York: Harworth Pastoral Press, 1994); Marianne Habersetzer, *Leben und Glauben–ein katechetischer Weg mit älteren Menschen* (Würzburg: Echter, 1998); Ulrich Moser, *Identität, Spiritualität und Lebenssinn. Grundlagen seelsorgerlicher Begleitung im Altenheim* (Würzburg: Echter, 2000).

[25]See the beginning of this chapter.

[26]Koenig, *Aging and God*.

[27]Koenig, *Aging and God*, 284–94.

[28]See statements earlier in this chapter from the works of Martina Blasberg-Kuhnke (notes 5 and 20).

[29]See Alfons Auer, *Geglücktes Altern. Eine theologisch-ethische Ermutigung* (Freiburg: Herder, 1995), 109.

[30]Daniel Levinson, *The Seasons of a Man's Life* (New York: Knopf, 1978), 97.

[31]The now classic study is Philippe Ariès, *Western Attitudes Toward Death: From the Middle Ages to the Present* (Baltimore: Johns Hopkins Univ. Press, 1975); see also Joachim Wittkowski, *Psychologie des Todes* (Darmstadt: Wissenschaftliche Buchgesellschaft, 1990).

[32]Elisabeth Kübler-Ross, *On Death and Dying* (New York: Macmillan, 1969).

Chapter 7: Theological Demands on Postmodern Life

[1]The major exception in Germany is Albrecht Grözinger, *Die Kirche–ist sie noch zu retten? Anstiftungen für das Christentum in postmoderner Gesellschaft* (Gütersloh: Gütersloher Verlagshaus, 1998); for an overview on the German literature, see Wolfgang Steck, *Praktische Theologie. Horizonte der Religion, Konturen des neuzeitlichen Christentums, Strukturen der religiösen Lebenswelt*, vol. 1 (Stuttgart: Kohlhammer, 2000), 29ff.

[2]See Walter Brueggemann, *Texts under Negotiation: The Bible and Postmodern Imagination* (Minneapolis: Fortress, 1993); or the collections: David Ray Griffin, William A. Beardslee, and Joe Holland, *Varieties of Postmodern Theology* (Albany, N.Y.: State Univ. of New York Press, 1989); Terrence R. Tilley, ed., *Postmodern Theologies: The Challenge of Religious Diversity* (New York: Maryknoll, 1995). To mention a few additional examples from Germany: Bernd Beuscher, *Positives Paradox. Entwurf einer neostrukturalistischen Religionspädagogik* (Vienna: Passagen, 1993); Hermann Kochanek, ed., *Religion und Glaube in der Postmoderne* (Nettetal: Steyler, 1996).

[3]David Harvey, *The Condition of Postmodernity: An Enquiry into the Origins of Cultural Change* (Oxford: Basil Blackwell, 1989); Wolfgang Welsch, *Unsere postmoderne Moderne* (Weinheim: VCH, 1988).

[4]Werner Helsper, "Das 'postmoderne Selbst'–ein neuer Subjekt-und Jugendmythos? Reflexionen anhand religiöser jugendlicher Orientierungen," in *Identitätsarbeit heute. Klassische und aktuelle Perspektiven der Identitätsforschung*, ed. Heiner Keupp and Renate Höfer (Frankfurt am Main: Suhrkamp, 1997), 174–206.

[5]See my earlier books: Friedrich Schweitzer, *Lebensgeschichte und Religion. Religiöse Entwicklung und Erziehung im Kindes- und Jugendalter* (Munich: Kaiser, 1987); idem, *Die Suche nach eigenem Glauben. Einführung in die Religionspädagogik des Jugendalters* (Gütersloh: Gütersloher Verlagshaus, 1996); idem, *Das Recht des Kindes auf Religion* (Gütersloh: Gütersloher Verlagshaus, 2000).

[6]Donald Capps, *Pastoral Care: A Thematic Approach* (Philadelphia: Westminster Press, 1979); John J. Gleason, *Growing Up to God: Eight Steps in Religious Development* (Nashville: Abingdon, 1975); Joachim Scharfenberg, *Einführung in die Pastoralpsychologie* (Göttingen: Vandenhoeck & Ruprecht, 1985).

[7]For a discussion, see Wilhelm Gräb, *Lebensgeschichten, Lebensentwürfe, Sinndeutungen. Eine Praktische Theologie gelebter Religion* (Gütersloh: Gütersloher Verlagshaus, 1998).

[8]Ulrich Beck, Anthony Giddens, and Scott Lash, *Reflexive Modernization: Politics, Tradition and Aesthetics in the Modern Social Order* (Stanford: Stanford Univ. Press, 1994).

[9]Schleiermacher's clearest statement on modernity can be found in his *On Religion: Speeches to Its Cultured Despisers* (New York: Harper & Row, 1958, orig. pub. 1799). For his view of practical theology, see idem, *Brief Outline on the Study of Theology*, trans. Terrence N. Tice (Atlanta: John Knox Press, 1966).

[10]For this understanding, see Volker Drehsen, *Neuzeitliche Konstitutionsbedingungen der Praktischen Theologie. Aspekte der theologischen Wende zur sozialkulturellen Lebenswelt christlicher Religion*. 2 vols. (Gütersloh: Gütersloher Verlagshaus, 1988); for the contemporary discussion, see Friedrich Schweitzer and Johannes A. van der Ven, eds., *Practical Theology—International Perspectives* (Frankfurt am Main: P. Lang, 1999).

[11]See the literature on postmodernity: Harvey, *The Condition of Postmodernity;* Welsch, *Unsere postmoderne Moderne;* Beck, Giddens, and Lash, *Reflexive Modernization*.

[12]For a more detailed discussion of these different forms of religion, see Dietrich Rössler, *Grundriß der Praktischen Theologie* (Berlin: De Gruyter, 1986).

[13]See José Casanova, *Public Religions in the Modern World* (Chicago: Univ. of Chicago Press, 1994).

[14]For further background information, see Schweitzer and van der Ven. eds., *Practical Theology;* Don S. Browning, ed., *Practical Theology* (San Francisco: Harper & Row, 1983); idem, *A Fundamental Practical Theology: Descriptive and Strategy Proposals* (Minneapolis: Fortress Press, 1991).

[15]Thomas S. Kuhn, *The Structure of Scientific Revolutions* (Chicago: Univ. of Chicago Press, 1966).

[16]For an example from the older literature, see Romano Guardini, *Die Lebensalter. Ihre ethische und pädagogische Bedeutung* (Würzburg: Werkbund-Verlag, no year of publication, approx. 1955).

[17]Many of them have been quoted in the chapters above.

[18]James E. Loder, *The Logic of the Spirit: Human Development in Theological Perspective* (San Francisco: Jossey-Bass, 1998).

[19]The chart is taken from my book, Friederich Schweitzer, *Lebensgeschichte und Religion. Religiöse Entwicklung und Erziehung im Kindes- und Jugendalter*, enlarged ed. (Gütersloh: Gütersloher Verlagshaus, 1999), 202. It is based on the earlier correlational efforts by Gleason, *Growing Up to God;* Joachim Scharfenberg, "Menschliche Reifung und christliche Symbole," in *Concilium* 14 (1978): 86–92; Donald Capps, *Pastoral Care*, 114; Heinz Müller-Pozzi, "Gott–Erbe des verlorenen Pardieses. Ursprung und Wesen der Gotteside im Lichte psychoanalytischer Konzepte," in *Wege zum Menschen* 33 (1981): 190–203; J. Eugene Wright, *Erikson: Identity and Religion* (New York: Seabury Press, 1982), 160; Hans-Jürgen Fraas, *Glaube und Identität. Grundlegung einer Didaktik religiöser Lernprozesse* (Göttingen: Vandenhoeck & Ruprecht, 1983), 107ff.; Peter Biehl, "Symbol und Metapher auf dem Weg zu einer religionspädagogischen Theorie religiöser Sprache," in *Jahrbuch der Religionspädagogik* 1 (1985): 54ff.

[20]Erik H. Erikson, *Insight and Responsibility: Lectures on the Ethical Implications of Psychoanalytic Insight* (New York: Norton, 1964), 111–34.

[21]Carol Gilligan, *In a Different Voice: Psychological Theory and Women's Development* (Cambridge: Harvard Univ. Press, 1982).